Trout Fishing
in
Southeast Minnesota

To My ~~Friends~~ Mike and Jane —
You have carved out the
prettiest spot in the middle of
my favorite place on earth.
I'm thrilled to have you as
neighbors! I wish you the very
best —

The Highweather Guide To

Trout Fishing
in
Southeast Minnesota

SECOND EDITION

*A Selective Guide to
the Streams and Rivers of
Minnesota's Bluff Country*

JOHN VAN VLIET

The Highweather Press
MINNEAPOLIS

Published by:
The Highweather Press, LLC
Post Office Box 24624
Minneapolis, MN 55424

ISBN 0-9632344-3-9

Unless otherwise stated, the maps in this book are taken from the Minnesota Department of Transportation maps for the following counties: Fillmore, Goodhue, Houston, Olmsted, Wabasha and Winona.

Jacket map is from the United States Geologic Survey, Elba Quadrangle, Minnesota.

Cover design and illustrations by Brad Springer
Front and back cover photographs by Phil Aarrestad
Book design by the author

DEDICATION

To Karen for her love, patience, support
and understanding.

To Paul and Caroline with love.

And to the memory of my father,
Willem Frederick van Vliet,
who was the best fishing companion I'll ever know.

ACKNOWLEDGMENTS

N o book of this kind is the work of just one person. I am very grateful for the generous contributions of many people. Though I have attempted to list them all below, I am sure I have forgotten at least another dozen equally important and generous folks, and I apologize for their omission.

My thanks to Phil Aarrestad, Mike Alwin, Wayne Bartz, Rich Belanger, Gordon & Julie Bentley, Jon Berdahl, Dan Callahan, Cy DeCosse, Mark Ebbers, Sheila Gebhardt, John Goplin, Tom Helgeson, Jim Humphrey, Duke Hust, Don Leeper, Bob Jacklin, Jan Jancourt, Tim Joseph, Bob & Jean Mitchell, Paul Mueller, Ross Mueller, Dave & Chad Peterson, John Randolph, Tom Rosenbauer, Joel Schultz, Ryan Shadrin, Bill Shogren, Alan Spaulding & Spaulding Angling Specialties, Brad Springer and Kurt Weieneth.

CONTENTS

PREFACE TO THE
SECOND EDITION

When I first saw the rugged valleys and sparkling streams of the southeast more than twenty years ago, their beauty seemed timeless and unchanging. Even after many years of fishing here, I saw little change from year to year. Sure, floods would scour a stream or two each season, a farm would change hands, and a fast-food restaurant would appear on the edge of a small town. But the sense of traveling back in time always greeted me when I returned to the southeast.

In the relatively short span of the last six years, however, it seems as if every stream, valley, road and small town has changed in some way – some greatly, others almost imperceptibly except, perhaps, to me.

These changes made it impossible simply to reprint the first edition one more time; I would have to revise. Then, as I began, I realized there were several fine streams I'd left out of the first edition that would have to be a part of any revision. I also wanted to add a few simple tips on fishing these, or any, small streams; a section on flies for the southeast; and the recipes for a handful of productive fly patterns. The revision became a thorough rewrite, and a greatly expanded new book.

But not everything changed; as I wrote in the preface to the first edition, "There are no fabled rivers here; no expensive fishing gear bears the name of a southeast Minnesota river." And that's still true today. There remains a feeling of solitude and abundance. And the fishing is still great.

Shortly after the first edition of this book was published six years ago, Robert Redford released the film *A River Runs Through It*, based on the book by Norman Maclean, and fly fishing burst into the national consciousness. Fly shops sprang up like wildflowers, land values along trout streams soared, and trout waters everywhere were crowded with enthusiastic newcomers to the sport.

But, despite the popularity of fly fishing nationwide, the trout streams of southeastern Minnesota remained largely undiscovered.

If I was concerned six years ago that *my* slender book would cause a stampede to the streams of the southeast, I was giving myself too much credit. While it was clear that there were a few more anglers on these streams after my book appeared, chances are it was Redford's movie that brought them out. The purpose of the first edition of this book was simply to introduce trout anglers to a variety of fishing opportunities in the southeast. In retrospect, its effect may also have been to spread the many trout anglers around, and even take some of the pressure off the more popular – though not necessarily better – streams. And that is the purpose of this new edition, as well.

So, if you have never fished the southeast, or are simply interested in finding some new trout water, I hope you'll take this guide along. It's my hope that you'll explore the southeast a bit and discover the beauty here. I'm confident that you'll find a favorite stream and return, as I do, season after season, year after year.

I'll see you on the water.

John van Vliet
Minneapolis 1997

PART 1

INTRODUCTION TO SOUTHEAST MINNESOTA'S TROUT STREAMS

I

INTRODUCTION

THE GEOLOGY OF THE SOUTHEAST

Mention trout fishing and cold spring creeks in Minnesota and you're likely to get stares. To most people, Minnesota is synonymous with lakes. Images of the state's pine-fringed waters are used to entice the throngs of tourists who visit the countless fishing resorts across the central and northern parts of the state each year. So it is difficult for anyone who has never been to southeastern Minnesota to imagine there is a corner of the state that can be described as having hundreds of miles of water, yet virtually no lakes. The southeast's towering limestone bluffs, deep valleys, cold rushing streams, wild turkeys and rattlesnakes may conjure up images of the Smoky mountains, the Ozarks or the Black Hills. Yet even those places are dotted with lakes. So what accounts for this anomaly in the land of 10,000 lakes? Part of the answer lies in the unpredictability of ice.

Ten thousand years ago, the last of four major ice advances – the Wisconsin – receded slowly toward Hudson Bay and the Arctic Circle, leaving behind a vastly altered landscape. But, like the previous three glacial periods (the Illinoisian, the Kansan and the Nebraskan), whose fingers of ice had reached as far south as Kansas, this ice sheet had inexplicably split in its advance and flowed around a 10,000-square-mile area of sedimentary rock in the upper Midwest. When the ice was gone, this island of rocky uplands covering parts of Wisconsin, Illinois, Minnesota and Iowa, did not resemble the vast and scoured plains surrounding it. Spared the grating effects of the ice, it retained the landscape common to uplifted areas of former sea bottom: deeply eroded strata of limestone.

Geologists who studied the northern European landscape centuries ago attributed glacial features – moraines, eskers, drumlins and the like – to the effects of water, and called them "drift," the remnants of what these geologists imagined were floods of biblical proportions. The name stuck, and the term "glacial drift" later was applied to features on the landscape left by glaciation. But geologists found no such glacial features in this unique region of the Midwest, so they called it the "Driftless Area."

From the porous limestone strata of this driftless area, and fed by the melting glaciers, flowed streams that carved deep valleys in the soft sedimentary rock as they sought the level of the Mississippi River, which bisects the region.

Water percolating into and through the limestone strata carried minerals that dissolved the limestone and created voids or cavities in the strata. As the groundwater levels dropped, some of these voids collapsed forming sinkholes, which dot the landscape throughout the region and are easiest to find around the town of Fountain (p. 66). Many of these voids survived as caverns, some of which have become popular tourist stops in Minnesota and Wisconsin. Countless others remain undiscovered and unexplored.

Where you find this limestone, or *karst*, topography, you generally find limestone spring creeks and, if you're lucky, trout. Similar regions exist in Appalachia, Pennsylvania, southern England and New Zealand, to name a few. The constant water temperatures (generally 50 to 55°F) provide sufficiently cool temperatures to support trout through the hot summers and keep the streams free of ice in the harsh Minnesota winters. The limestone produces the relatively high alkalinity required to sustain the critical biomass: aquatic plants, insects and invertebrates essential to trout.

Today, the Driftless Area remains an island of deep valleys, wooded bluffs, limestone caverns and rushing streams in a sea of Midwestern farmland, and makes up one of the highest concentrations of spring creeks in North America.

It may not be what the tourists think of when you mention Minnesota, but to trout anglers, the southeast remains a unique and welcome vestige of the ice age.

TROUT OF THE REGION

In addition to their effect on the landscape, glaciers also had an influence on the distribution of the only salmonid native* to the southeast: the brook trout. The Wisconsin ice advance pushed the brookie south from its sub-arctic range across Labrador and Quebec, leaving small remnant populations as far south as Georgia, Tennessee, Kentucky and the Carolinas. Similarly, it's generally believed that a few brook trout populations survived in the Driftless Area west of the Mississippi, within the watersheds of the Upper Iowa, Yellow and Root Rivers. This region represents the extreme western limit of the brook trout's native range.

The brook trout is not a true trout, but rather a charr, a close relative to the lake trout and Arctic charr. It is also

---

* A "native" fish is defined as one, stocked or wild, in its original geographic range; "wild" describes a fish that is the result of natural reproduction in the stream. The offspring of stocked fish are considered wild.

known as the eastern speckled trout, American brook trout and squaretail, and its Latin name, *Salvelinus fontinalis*, literally means "charr living in springs." Unfortunately, the brook trout that are found in southeast streams today are the result of stocking, not native populations.

Brook trout are easily identified by a number of features, most notably the light-colored spots and vermiculations on the darker background color of the back and sides of the fish, and bright white margins on the leading edges of the lower fins. They may reach two pounds in the southeast, although they usually weigh much less and are most commonly 6- to 10-inches long.

Brown trout (*Salmo trutta*) have been stocked in the southeast since the late 1880s. Eggs were brought over from Germany in 1884 and from Scotland a year later, and both were widely distributed in American waters by the turn of the century. Brown trout adapted well to the small, swift streams of the southeast and have become the dominant species in the region.

Several strains of brown trout live here, but all are recognizable by the presence of dark spots on a lighter background. Brown trout can grow substantially larger than brook trout in these rivers, some exceeding twelve pounds. Most, however, are in the 10- to 14-inch range.

Rainbow trout (*Onchorhynchus mykiss*) have been periodically stocked in southeast streams since the 1880s, but they tend to be caught quickly or migrate downstream. Unfortunately, a downstream migration in the southeast usually means becoming a meal for warm-water fishes in the waters of the lower stretches and in the Mississippi.

Rainbows historically were stocked just before trout opener to provide sport in the early season, but stream improvements have increased the numbers of wild trout – brookies and browns – and reduced the need for stocking.

Rainbows are distinguished by the red stripe along their lateral line, and have dark spots on a light background.

They often appear silvery in these streams. Rainbows occasionally carry over from season to season and some weighing over eight pounds have been taken.

FISHING REGULATIONS

The State of Minnesota requires that you purchase a trout stamp in addition to your fishing license if you plan to fish for trout. You can purchase a license in nearly every gas station and hardware store, as well as fishing stores, throughout the southeast. In addition to the regular fishing regulations, some streams in the southeast are subject to special regulations. These special regulations are usually posted along those streams subject to such regs, but check the booklet that comes with your license for specific special regulations.

PRIVATE AND PUBLIC

The state has been acquiring property and easements along the streams and rivers of the southeast for decades. However, much of the land along the rivers remains privately owned. It is best to ask permission from the landowners before fishing the streams that run through their property. As a rule, state and county routes that cross these streams are legal access points and in most cases, if you stay between the high-water marks on each riverbank, you should have no trouble. There are exceptions, however, where landowners vigorously enforce their posted boundaries, ignoring recreational-use laws, so it is always advisable to seek permission and respect all no trespassing signs.

Below is the Department of Natural Resources' own language concerning the current trespass law:

> The trespass law now applies to all outdoor recreation. Whether fishing, hunting, or taking part in any other outdoor recreation, you may not enter legally posted land or agri-

cultural land without permission.

Landowners, lessees, or authorized managers need only post their land once a year. The signs must be placed at intervals of 1,000 feet (500 feet in wooded areas) or signs may be placed at primary corners and at access points to the property. Signs must state "No Trespassing," or similar words, in 2-inch-high letters and have the signature or name and telephone number of the landowner, lessee, or manager.

There can be civil and criminal penalties for violation of the trespass laws. Civil penalties start with $50 for first offense and up to $500 and loss of license or registration for a third offense within three years. All conservation and peace officers enforce trespass laws.

Rules of Thumb for Water Access and Recreational Use:

These are simple rules of thumb and are not intended to address all water access and recreational use situations. If you have doubts about whether you may be trespassing on private land, we recommend that you ask the landowner for permission.

1. *What is lawful access?*

A stream or lake is lawfully accessible if there is a public access, or if public land or a public road right-of-way abuts the surface of the water, or if you have permission to cross private land to reach the surface of the water.

2. *What is recreational use?*

Recreational use includes boating, swimming, fishing, hunting, trapping, and similar activities. It includes walking in the water in connection with such activities regardless of who owns the land beneath the surface of the water.

3. *What waters are open to recreational use?*

A stream or lake is open to recreational use over its entire surface if it is capable of recreational use and if it is lawfully accessible. Any water that will float a canoe is capable of recreational use, but other waters may also qualify depending upon the circumstances.

When in doubt, ask permission.

CAMPING IN THE SOUTHEAST

If you plan to camp in southeastern Minnesota, you should have no trouble finding a good place to pitch your tent. I have included directions to five Minnesota state parks that offer excellent facilities and, in all but two of the parks, direct access to great fishing. It's wise to call ahead, especially if you plan to camp over a weekend. The state park toll-free reservation number is listed in the appendix, as are the numbers for the individual parks. In addition to the state parks, there are many other fine campgrounds in the area. For a listing of these, contact the Minnesota Office of Tourism, whose number also is listed in the appendix.

A WORD ABOUT THE MAPS IN THIS BOOK

This guide is intended to be used in conjunction with the excellent map available free of charge from the Minnesota Department of Natural Resources (DNR). The DNR map, entitled "Trout Streams of Southeast Minnesota," is an assemblage of the Minnesota Department of Transportation (DOT) maps, with colored lines added to indicate stretches of trout water. The DNR and DOT maps are not perfect, but they give a good overview of virtually every passable road in each county at the time of the last survey. Changes do occur over time, however, and these maps cannot be considered completely accurate.

Another problem with the DOT maps is that they do not show the topographical relief of the area. I have found it very helpful to pick up a copy of the USGS topographical map of a specific area when I am planning to explore a stream in detail. In addition to roads, streams and relief, these topo maps give an indication of which areas are wooded and which are not. They also display symbols representing houses, which can sometimes help you locate landowners.

23

In order to be consistent with the DNR trout-stream map, most of the maps in this book are taken from the DOT maps. If you wish to buy the DOT and USGS maps, you can find them at one of the handful of good map stores in the Twin Cities. The camping outfitter stores in Rochester carry the USGS maps, as well.

The DNR/DOT maps include printed gridlines representing the sections of the Township and Range lines of the land survey. In other words, each square represents one square mile. This can give you a good idea of distances on a relatively straight road or stream. But remember, a meandering meadow creek and a flying crow measure distances very differently.

Many anglers rely on the DeLorme *Minnesota Atlas and Gazetteer* for guidance. These excellent map books are inexpensive and provide a good overview of every corner of the state. However, I find the scale just a little too large for pinpointing individual streams and accesses. I recommend keeping a copy of the *Atlas and Gazetteer* in your car, but take along the county and DNR maps as well.

AND FINALLY. . .

One warm, bright morning almost seven years ago, I was fishing in the southeast with my friend, J.B. We were working a section of stream that is his favorite. It's a beautiful place at the foot of a high limestone bluff where the river runs through fast riffles, lingers in deep pools, and is filled with trophy brown trout.

As we paused midstream, the river still in deep shadow and a mist drifting on the pools, I mentioned to J.B. that I was writing a guide to trout fishing in the southeast. He looked at me in horror. "You're not going to tell anyone about this place, are you?" he implored.

The truth is, with so many miles of trout streams in a region, a book of this size can be neither comprehensive nor exhaustive. This book is intended simply to introduce you to the southeast and to help you find your way to a variety of fine trout streams. The rest is up to you.

J.B.'s favorite place is here, of course. But you'll just have to find it for yourself.

II
CHOOSING THE RIGHT TACKLE

No one can tell you which equipment to choose, just as no one can tell you which car to drive or which house to buy. Selecting fly tackle is clearly a personal decision based on such factors as experience, skill level, casting style, and budget. But one of the keys to fly-fishing success is tailoring your tackle to the conditions you are likely to encounter. The following are a few guidelines to help you choose the right gear for a trip to the streams of the southeast.

FLY RODS

The primary factors to consider when choosing a rod are the size of the water you're likely to encounter, the distance you'll need to cast, the size of the flies you'll be casting and the size fish you're after.

The majority of the streams in the southeast are shallow or narrow, or both. By July, the bankside weeds have grown taller than the height of most anglers. Wooded sections often have a low, overhanging canopy of leaves. Streams that run through grazed pasture land leave you no place to hide from the unblinking and ever-wary eyes of trout. To wade these streams armed with a 9-foot, 7-weight rod would be like going after quail with a 10-gauge shotgun. Sure, you might get something, but you've given the quarry an unnecessary advantage – or a grave disadvantage. Long rods and heavy lines make it difficult to deliver small flies to spooky trout with stealth and finesse. And if you do hook a fish, the heavy rod makes for a lopsided fight.

Light-line rods, such as those in the 1- to 4-weight range, are all you need to deliver small flies short distances. Short rods, in the 7- to 8-foot range, let you keep your casts low and focused. And the fish are less likely to see a short rod waving overhead than a long one. Sure, a 9-foot rod helps you lift your backcast over tall weeds and is great for "dapping," the technique of dangling a fly on a short length of line causing it to dance on the surface, but the advantages of a shorter rod outweigh the disadvantages.

If you're fishing with tiny Blue-winged Olives, Tricos or any number of small nymphs, all the more reason to leave the long, heavyweight rods at home. On the other hand, heavily weighted nymphs, Wooly Buggers or large grasshopper patterns will tax your 3-weight rod. If you're fishing large, weighted or wind-resistant flies, a 5- or 6-weight rod might be a better choice.

The last factor in rod selection is the size of the fish

you're likely to encounter, and let's be honest: the vast majority of fish here are not trophies. There are many days when you'll catch 10-inch browns until you think that's all there are in the water. But every now and then you'll connect with something that tugs once, shakes its unseen head with authority, and parts your leader in the middle. Either way, I'd rather be armed for the small fish than the large. You can land a big fish on small tackle; but can you fool a bunch of smaller fish with big tackle? The choice, as I've said, is yours.

So what rod should you choose? Start with my recommendation of a 8-foot 4-weight and then use your own judgment. If you only own one rod and it's a 7-weight, don't run out and buy a new rod just because I told you to use a 4-weight. But if you've been looking for an excuse to buy a new rod, I just gave you one.

FLY LINES

Which fly line you choose is determined in large part by the type and size of the fly you're casting, the distance you're casting and the type of casts you make. If this sounds familiar, it's because these are many of the same factors that determined which rod you selected. The question here isn't what line *weight* to choose; you made that choice when you selected your rod. (A 4-weight rod, as you know, is designed to cast a 4-weight line.) The real question is which *taper* to buy. Taper is the variation in thickness of the fly line's coating along the length of the line, and generally determines how a line will perform. (Remember, it's the weight of the fly line that distinguishes fly fishing from all other forms of fishing. The line propels the weightless fly and allows you to control the fly on or in the water. This variation in thickness, or taper, of the fly-line coating is the basis of fly casting and line control.) The two primary fly-line tapers to consider for fishing the small streams of the southeast are weight-forward and double-taper.

Weight-forward lines are designed with most of their weight in the first 30 feet (roughly one-third of the line's overall length), tapering to a thinner section, called *running line*, which makes up the remainder of the line. Weight-forward lines are superior for casting greater distances, punching flies into the wind, or throwing heavier flies.

Double-taper lines have a long midsection, called the *belly*, with identical tapers at each end of the line. They cast well at short to medium distances and, because they don't have the transition to running line at 30 feet that can cause a weight-forward line to "hinge," they are excellent for roll-casting. Double-tapers seem to have a more delicate presentation, a real advantage when fishing small streams with small flies. But perhaps the greatest advantage of double-tapers is that they are essentially two fly lines in one: if the line wears out or is damaged at one end, you can simply turn it around rather than replace it.

Though the two types of line tapers are practically indistinguishable over their first 30 feet, I prefer double-taper lines for their versatility and roll-casting. If in doubt, ask your local fly shop to let you cast one of each style in a variety of conditions and decide for yourself.

Another factor to consider in choosing a line is buoyancy. Today's fly lines are designed to float high on the water or sink at a specific rate. While sinking lines have their uses, stick with floating lines for fishing southeastern Minnesota.

The last factor in choosing a fly line is color. The most popular colors of fly line are light or fluorescent. While these colors are easy for the angler to see in the air and on the water, some people feel they can spook the fish. Some manufacturers produce lines in subtle grays, sometimes called "spring creek" lines, and I happen to prefer these gray lines. But, in most cases, the long leader is sufficient to keep the tip of the fly line out of the fish's vision, making fly-line color unimportant.

LEADERS & TIPPETS

The connection between fly line and fly is one of the most overlooked factors in fly fishing. A good leader not only forms this transparent link between fly line and fly, it also helps transfer the energy of the cast smoothly and efficiently, and can give the fly the critical lifelike action on or in the water. Your leader must taper down from a fairly heavy butt section, which is attached to your fly line, to a fine-diameter section called the tippet, to which the fly is attached.

For the small, clear streams of the southeast, the longer and finer the leader the better. Start with a standard, 9-foot tapered leader. Snip off a foot or so of the tip of the leader and add a couple of feet of single-diameter tippet material, the kind that comes on the narrow plastic spools. The smaller the diameter (or X-rating), the better.

Bear in mind that the X-rating of a tippet simply indicates diameter, not breaking strength. All 6X tippets, for example, are .005". But, depending on the manufacturer, the breaking strength of 6X tippets can vary from 1.4- to 3.5-pound test.

Switching to a smaller-diameter tippet almost always results in more fish caught – especially on clear creeks. Give plenty of thought to your leader, and experiment with several different brands.

REELS

I wrote once that calling a reel just a place to store line is like saying a car's brake pedal is just a place to rest your foot. But on the small streams of the southeast, a reel really *is* just a place to store line.

Of course, there are advantages and disadvantages to the different types of reels you're likely to encounter at the fly shop, but the fish we're after aren't going to demand a

Trout Fishing

high-tech drag, anti-reverse reel or high-capacity backing storage. And if the fish you catch here *do*, call me; we'll fish *your* favorite spot instead of mine.

For the southeast streams, select a reel that is designed for the rod and line weight you're using. A single-action, ratchet-and-pawl reel is sufficient for all but the rarest fish.

Of course, that said, I'll admit that a small disc-drag reel with a smooth, imperceptible take-up is ideal for protecting the light tippets I described above, but let's be realistic: I'm more likely to lose a fish because I step on my line or wrap it around my knuckle, than to lose one because of a slight take-up bump on my little ratchet-and-pawl reel.

WADING GEAR

One of the most often asked questions from anglers who have never fished the southeast is: "Should I bring hip boots or chest waders?"

Your choice of wading gear depends mainly on the depth and temperature of the water.

Most southeast streams can be fished easily with hip boots. I like hippers because they're quick and easy to pull on, comfortable to walk in, and generally inexpensive to replace when they're worn out. Unfortunately, there are always those two or three occasions on every trip where the biggest fish is just beyond the wading depth of your hippers.

Chest waders give you access to more water, but can be hot and uncomfortable to walk in for long distances.

A good compromise is the breathable chest wader, which uses Gore-Tex, or similar material, to allow perspiration to escape while keeping you dry. Their single disadvantage is their cost, which can be prohibitively high. Those who have switched to breathables, however, would never switch back.

Lastly, leave your neoprene chest waders at home, unless you are fishing the winter season or early spring.

32

MISCELLANEOUS

Other essential items include: lightweight rain gear that can be stowed easily in the pouch of your vest, a compass for navigating the nameless and numberless backroads, a snake-bite kit for the unlikely encounter with one of the rare timber rattlers that inhabit the bluffs, and a weather radio to help you stay abreast of any severe weather that may develop beyond the limited horizons of the deep valleys.

III
NATURALS & ARTIFICIALS

Trout spend their lives pursuing their next meal. In streams, they rely on the current to provide a steady supply of aquatic insects and other foods, such as minnows, leeches and crustaceans, as well as terrestrial insects. Of these foods, aquatic insects make up the largest portion of a trout's diet. The four main groups of aquatic insects include mayflies (*Ephemeroptera*), caddisflies (*Trichoptera*), stoneflies (*Plecoptera*) and midges (*Diptera*). Though "hatches," the emergence of the adult forms of aquatic insects, occur only sporadically throughout the season, the immature forms of these insects (larvae, pupae and nymphs) are present all year long. These immature forms make up as much as ninety percent of a trout's diet. And though trout often feed opportunistically, it's their aggravating tendency to feed extremely selectively that has earned them their reputation as an "intelligent" gamefish.

When trout are feeding selectively, such as during a heavy insect hatch, it's important to have a fly pattern that

Trout Fishing

closely imitates the particular stage, size, shape, color and action of the natural. The hatch charts below do not include every individual species of insect found in the streams of the southeast; rather, they are designed to help you identify which insects you're likely to encounter throughout the season, and which fly pattern best imitates a particular insect. Conversely, not all the aquatic insects listed on the hatch charts are present in all streams, but these charts should give you a fairly good idea which patterns to stock up on before you go.

36

MAYFLIES

SPECIES	COMMON NAME OR IMITATION	SIZE	April	May	June	July	August	Sept.
Baetis vagans, intercalaris, others	Blue-wing Olive (BWO) Tiny BWO	16-22	■	■	■		■	■
Ephemerella subvaria	Dark Hendrickson	12-14	■	■				
Paraleptophlebia adoptiva & mollis	Blue Quill Blue Dun	16-18		■	■			
Ephemerella invaria & rotunda	Light Hendrickson Sulphur Duns	14-16		■	■			
Stenonema vicarium & fuscum	March Brown Gray Fox	10-16			■	■		
Stenonema ithaca	Light Cahill	10-16			■	■		
Tricorythodes	Trico	20-28				■	■	■
Pseudocloëon anoka & others	Blue-wing Olive	20-28			■	■	■	■
Ephemerella dorothea	Sulphur Eastern Pale Even. Dun	16-18		■	■			
Hexagenia limbata	Hex Giant Michigan Mayfly	6-10			■	■		

(Month)

CADDISFLIES

Species	Common Name or Imitation	Size	April	May	June	July	August	Sept.
					Month			
Brachycentrus spp	Grannum Caddis (Tube-case maker)	14-16	■	■	■	■	■	
Chimarra sp	Little Black Caddis (Sedge) (Net-spinning caddis)	16-20	■	■	■		■	
Hydropsyche sp	Spotted Sedge (Net-spinning caddis)	14-16		■	■	■	■	
Hydroptilidae spp	Microcaddis (Purse-case maker)	18-22	■	■	■	■	■	■
Glossosomatidae	Tan Sedge (Saddle-case maker)	14-16		■	■	■	■	
Leptoceridae	Longhorn Sedge (Net-spinning caddis)	14-18			■	■	■	

STONEFLIES & MIDGES

SPECIES	COMMON NAME OR IMITATION	SIZE	April	May	June	July	August	Sept.
					MONTH			
Taeniopteryx	Early Brown Stonefly	10-12	▓	▓				
Pterynarcys spp	Giant Black	2-6	▓	▓				
Isoperla spp	Little Yellow Stone Yellow Sally	12-14		▓	▓	▓		
Midges	Tan, Gray, Olive, Yellow, Black	20-28	▓	▓	▓	▓	▓	▓

IV

SUGGESTED FLY PATTERNS FOR SOUTHEAST MINNESOTA

Certainly the most common question concerning the southeast is: "What flies should I carry?" Below is a list of what I consider essential patterns. Most of them are familiar old traditionals and available in any fly shop. A few, however, are variations that have proven effective. For this reason, I've included the recipes, along with a few personal notes and comments, for about half of the patterns. There are no photographs of the flies, but since most are variations on popular patterns, you'll have no trouble figuring out what they look like. (Consult the bibliography on page 126 for a list of books on flies and fly tying.)

This is by no means a complete list of flies. Check with the local fly shops and guides for current information and advice on hatches, patterns and general stream conditions, which often dictate the patterns you'll need.

SUGGESTED FLY PATTERNS

Pattern Name	*Size Range*

Dry Flies

Adams	14 - 22
Blue-wing Olive*	16 - 24
Elk-hair Caddis	12 - 18
Hendrickson*	12 - 18
Humpy	10 - 16
Light Cahill*	10 - 20
Little Black Caddis*	16 - 20
Little Yellow Stone*	12 - 16
Sulphur*	16 - 18
Trico Spinner*	22 - 26

Nymphs & Wet Flies

Deep Sparkle Pupa*	14 - 16
Gold-Ribbed Hare's Ear*	12 - 18
Partridge-and-Orange*	12 - 16
Pheasant tail*	12 - 18
Prince *Black*	12 - 20
Scud	10 - 16
Serendipity	16 - 22

Terrestrials

Ants	16 - 20
Beetles*	10 - 16
Inchworm	10 - 14
Jacklin's Hopper*	8 - 12

Streamers

Muddler Minnows	4 - 10
Wooly Buggers	4 - 10

*Indicates pattern with recipe provided on following pages.

V
SELECTED FLY RECIPES

DRY FLIES

One of the great joys and challenges of these, or any, spring creeks is fishing a dry fly. Though nymph fishermen will tell you that trout feed primarily on the immature forms of aquatic insects (generically called "nymphs"), dry-fly enthusiasts live for those times when the insects are in the air or on the water, and the fish are "looking up." Below are recipes for a handful of important patterns for southeast Minnesota.

Blue-wing Olive (BWO)

Hook: TMC 100; 12 to 22
Thread: Olive 6/0 to 8/0
Wing: Blue dun hen-hackle tips
Tail: Blue dun hackle fibers
Body: Olive beaver
Hackle: Blue dun

Notes:
This essential pattern imitates a number of common may-flies throughout the season, most notably the *Baetis* and *Pseudocloëon*. When in doubt, choose a fly of this pattern in a size or two smaller than the natural. Experiment with blend-ing shades of tan into the olive dubbing.

Light Cahill

Hook: TMC 100; 10 to 20
Thread: Cream 6/0 to 8/0
Wing: Lemon wood duck flank
Tail: Light ginger hackle fibers
Body: Cream beaver
Hackle: Light ginger

Notes:
A good early summer pattern, the Light Cahill imitates the *Stenonema ithaca* and other light-colored mayflies. Vary the shade of the body and hackle from white to ginger to match the natural, if necessary.

Hendrickson (Dark)

Hook:	TMC 100; 12 to 18
Thread:	Cream 6/0 to 8/0
Wing:	Lemon wood duck flank
Tail:	Medium to dark blue dun hackle fibers
Body:	Muskrat dubbing
Hackle:	Medium to dark blue dun

Notes:
One of the most anticipated hatches of the year – perhaps
because it's one of the first major hatches of the season – the
Hendrickson imitates the adult *Ephemerella subvaria*.
Unfortunately, Hendrickson hatches do not occur on all
streams in the southeast and vary in intensity from year to
year.

Sulphur

Hook:	TMC 100; 16 to 18
Thread:	Cream 6/0
Wing:	Cream hen-hackle tips
Tail:	Light blue dun hackle fibers
Body:	Cream fox
Hackle:	Light blue dun

Notes:
Locally, the Sulphur imitates the *Ephemerella dorothea*, also
known as the Eastern Pale Evening Dun. The true Sulphur
Duns are the *Ephemerella invaria* and *rotunda*, the latter of
which we call the Light Hendrickson. A significant and
ubiquitous hatch throughout the Midwest, the Sulphur is an
excellent late-day pattern from mid-May through June.

Trico Spinner

Hook:	TMC 100; 22 to 26
Thread:	Black 8/0
Wing:	White hen hackle tips or poly wing, spent style
Tail:	Dun hackle fibers, split
Body:	Black beaver

Notes:

Just when you think it's too hot to fish, or you're ready to switch to hoppers, the diminutive *Tricorythodes* emerge in clouds just after dawn and lure you back to the stream. Appearing from July through September, these tiny black-bodied, white-winged flies call for super-fine tippets and pinpoint casts – a tall order when the streamside vegetation is reaching full height.

Little Black Caddis

Hook:	TMC 102Y; 17 to 19. TMC 100; 18
Thread:	Black 8/0
Abdomen:	Black mole
Wing:	Gray raffia or Swiss Straw, caddis-style
Thorax:	Black mole
Hackle:	A collar of stiff black hackle

Notes:

A few remarkable and enjoyable hours on the water with Dr. Ross Mueller during the black caddis (*Chimarra*) hatch convinced me that his Little Black Caddis pattern is required tying for every angler who ventures out in April and May. Tie this pattern in several sizes to be safe. (See Ross Mueller's *Upper Midwest Flies that Catch Trout* for details on this and other effective Midwestern patterns.)

Little Yellow Stone (Yellow Sally)

Hook:	TMC 100; 12 to 16
Thread:	Yellow or cream 6/0
Tail:	Yellow deer or elk hair
Tag:	Red thread (optional)
Rib:	Ginger hackle palmered over body
Body:	Yellow floss
Wing:	Yellow deer or elk, caddis style
Hackle:	Ginger

Notes:

Watch for the naturals (of the genus *Isoperla*) in early to mid-summer. Also commonly known as the Yellow Sally, the Little Yellow Stone can be tied in shades ranging from cream or pale ginger to bright yellow.

NYMPHS & WET FLIES

I once wrote somewhere that dry flies make up the largest category of fly patterns. I'm not so sure anymore. New patterns appear in the magazines and fly catalogs practically every day. In my experience, however, there are just a handful of nymph patterns that work exceptionally well across a wide variety of conditions, and these form the foundation of nymphing. The following patterns are time-proven and deceptively simple. I wouldn't be caught without them.

Gold-Ribbed Hare's Ear

Hook:	TMC 3761; 12 to 18
Thread:	Tan or brown 6/0
Tail:	Hare's mask guard hair
Rib:	Fine oval or flat gold tinsel
	or copper wire
Abdomen:	Hare's mask
Wingcase:	Mottle turkey wing segment
Thorax:	Hare's mask, dubbed fatter than abdomen

Notes:

This popular pattern originated as a wet fly, but eventually lost its collar of soft hackle in favor of a more realistic wingcase. An excellent producer all season long, the Gold-Ribbed Hare's Ear works well both as an imitator and a searching pattern. Add a gold bead for weight and flash, if desired.

Pheasant-Tail Nymph

Hook: TMC 3761; 12 to 18
Thread: Brown 6/0
Tail: Ringneck pheasant-tail fibers
Rib: Fine copper wire
Abdomen: Pheasant-tail fibers, wrapped
Wingcase: Pheasant-tail
Thorax: Pheasant-tail or peacock herl

Notes:
Developed in England by the late Frank Sawyer, riverkeeper on the Wiltshire Avon for half a century, this pattern is truly one of the all-time greats. Sawyer used only the copper wire and pheasant tail – no thread, no peacock herl. I often tie it Sawyer-style, but I suggest using thread for ease of tying, and peacock, well, because fish can't resist it.

Deep Sparkle Pupa

Hook: TMC 2457 or 2487; 14 to 16
Thread: Brown 6/0
Overbody: Green Antron yarn, pulled over abdomen
            to form a veil
Abdomen: Green Antron, wrapped
Wing: Brown partridge fibers, tied in at sides
Head: Brown Antron or thread

Notes:
There are many good caddis pupa patterns available, but I have so many success stories with this brilliant pattern that it's far and away my favorite. It was developed by the legendary Gary LaFontaine, and discussed in detail in his fine book *Trout Flies, Proven Patterns*.

Partridge-And-Orange Soft-Hackle

Hook: TMC 100 or 3761; 12 to 16
Thread: Orange 6/0
Body: Orange floss
Thorax: Hare's mask (optional)
Hackle: A collar of brown or gray partridge

Notes:

I love all wet flies, especially soft-hackles, and this beautiful-ly simple pattern created by Sylvester Nemes is among my very favorites. It imitates emerging, stillborn or adult mayflies, and even craneflies. Substitute green or yellow floss and you'll begin to discover Syl's genius.

TERRESTRIALS

Don't wait for the heat of summer and hopper weather to switch to land-born insects, or terrestrials. The beetle pattern on page 52 works well throughout the season.

Jacklin's Hopper

Hook:	TMC 5212; 8 to 12
Thread:	Yellow or red 6/0
Tail:	Red deer hair (short)
Butt:	Fluorescent green Antron yarn
Rib:	Brown hackle palmered over body and trimmed
Body:	Fluorescent green Antron
Wing:	Natural gray goose or mottled turkey quill segment
Head:	Natural elk hair, bullet-style (tied in with tips facing forward, then pulled back), tips form collar

Notes:

There are many good hopper patterns out there – every well-known flytier has one – but I credit my friend and mentor Bob Jacklin with creating a hopper with the perfect combination of fishing success and ease of tying. Bob Jacklin is a quiet and unsung legend of Western fly fishing. A Yellowstone guide for more than thirty years, an expert fly-tier, a master fly caster, and a humble and soft-spoken man, Jacklin was the first, and for many years the only, person Lee Wulff trusted to tie his famous "Wulff" patterns commercially. He runs one of the oldest fly shops in West Yellowstone, Montana.

Deer Hair Beetle

Hook:	TMC 100; 10 to 16
Thread:	Black 6/0
Shellback:	Black deer hair, tied in at hook bend with tips facing back, then pulled forward over body and secured at head
Body:	Peacock Herl

Notes:

This simple pattern is effective under many different conditions throughout the year. Tie the peacock body as fat as possible. Snip two or three strands of the deer-hair shellback near the hook bend and allow these to stick out at the sides to create the illusion of legs. Add a small piece of fluorescent red or yellow yarn at the head for better visibility.

V

TEN TIPS FOR
SMALL-STREAM FISHING

The small streams of the Driftless Area present a unique set of challenges. Their extreme clarity, intimate size, and abundant vegetation can frustrate even the most experienced angler. But these streams reward those who approach carefully and who take time to observe their surroundings. Below are just a few suggestions to help you meet the challenges that spring creeks offer.

1. Approach With Care

Be prepared to wear out the knees of your waders. Small streams require a low, stealthy approach. A trout's wide window of vision, combined with the clear water, make it difficult to approach the water without spooking the fish. As a result, it's not unusual to see fly anglers casting while kneeling or crouched on the bank. I know one person who routinely approaches the stream bank on all fours with the rod held crosswise in his teeth like a dog with a bone. You may not have to go to this extreme, but it *is* important to keep a low profile.

2. Blend In

Wear clothing that blends in with the background of the stream environment. In early spring, wear tans and olives; as the summer approaches, shift to greens; and in the early fall, try a hunter's camouflage, such as Realtree. Traditional camouflage is effective all season long. Avoid wearing bright colors, especially whites. Choose a tan or green hat; a white hat will spook the fish before you even see them.

3. Seek The Shade

On sunny days, fish the shaded areas. That's where the fish are. Be careful to stay in the shadows as you approach a fish holding in a shady lie. If this isn't possible, keep the sun at your back.

4. Stay Off The Beaten Path

Don't be a slave to the trails along a stream. Chances are the fish have grown accustomed to anglers approaching from a certain direction. Fishing from the other side of the stream, the less frequently used side, will give you new angles to cast to wary or pressured fish.

5. Change Your Habits

Challenge yourself to fish at different times of the day. If you usually go to the stream in the evening, try it in the morning. You'll be surprised by the new things you'll learn.

6. Fish Fine and Far Off

Walton and Cotton were right: use the longest leader you can cast efficiently. Using a 12-foot leader will result in more caught fish than a 9-foot leader. And remember, a 6X tippet will allow you to fool more fish than a 5X.

7. *Try Terrestrials All Year*

Don't underestimate the effectiveness of terrestrial patterns. Most anglers only think of terrestrials, such as grasshoppers, in the slow, hot days of summer. But, beetle and ant imitations will catch trout from opening day to the last day of the season.

8. *Don't Come In Out Of The Rain*

There usually will be better hatches on rainy days than sunny ones. The exception to this is the hatch of the tricorythodes, which hatch more profusely on sunny mornings.

9. *Do A Little Bird Watching*

Watch the birds at streamside; their feeding and flight activity can tell you where the insects are. Hatches can be frustratingly isolated, sometimes occurring on one stretch of the stream and not on another only fifty yards away. Often the birds will betray the hatch.

10. *Practice Your Casting*

Casting accuracy probably is responsible for more "good" fishing days on a small stream than any other factor. It is more important to learn to cast a fly into a teacup at 20 feet than to learn to cast 80 feet of fly line.

PART 2

THE TROUT STREAMS OF THE SOUTHEAST

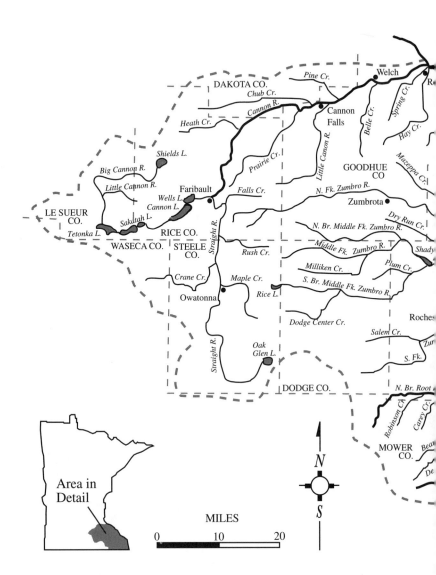

OVERALL MAP OF THE STREAMS AND RIVERS OF SOUTHEAST MINNESOTA

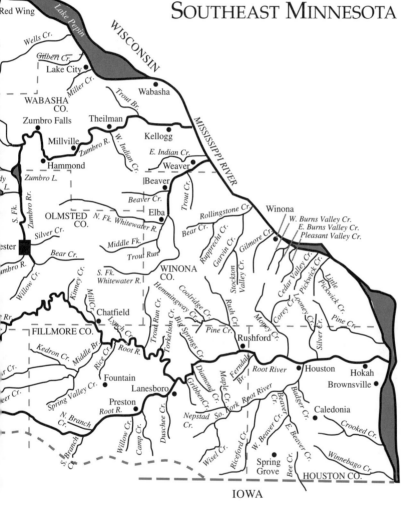

VI
AN ANGLER'S DRIVING TOUR

The 55 or so streams in this guide are divided into nine sections. Each section gives directions to a number of streams, leads the traveler from one stream to the next, and briefly describes each stream and its access and character. The itinerary of each section concludes with a state park or a town where you can eat, spend the night, or simply change out of your wading gear and head for home. If you don't have the time to explore all the streams included here in one trip, you may want to pick a section and follow the route to those streams, or choose the type of fishing you're interested in and use this guide to get to the streams you choose. But if you're ambitious, this book will take you on a guided tour of roughly 55 trout streams, and lead you through some beautiful countryside.

Our trip begins in Rochester, Minnesota, along east-west Interstate 90, and Highway 52, which runs north to the Twin Cities of Minneapolis and St. Paul, and south to Decorah, Iowa. There are plenty of places in and around Rochester to pick up a fishing license and trout stamp, buy a few flies or top off your Thermos.

Rochester stands at the head of three of the four major watersheds that flow east into the Mississippi River, draining the southeast: the Zumbro to the north, the Whitewater to the east, and the Root to the southeast of Rochester. The fourth major watershed in the southeast is the Cannon River, which flows east midway between Rochester and the Twin Cities. Of these four watersheds, the Whitewater and the Root River systems are considered the most productive trout fisheries. There are also a number of fine little streams that flow directly into the Mississippi between La Crescent and Red Wing.

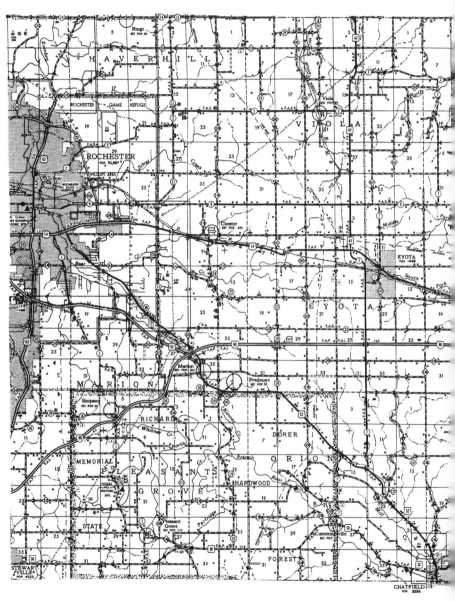

Map 1

SOUTH OF ROCHESTER

MILL CREEK • TROUT RUN CREEK • LYNCH CREEK •
RICE CREEK • SOUTH BRANCH OF THE ROOT RIVER •
SOUTH BRANCH CREEK (CANFIELD CREEK) •
NORTH BRANCH CREEK (FORESTVILLE CREEK)

Our first section takes us south on Route 52 out of Rochester toward the town of Chatfield (map 1). Just before Chatfield, Route 52 runs parallel to Mill Creek for a couple of miles. You can get to it in several places. In Chatfield, take Route 30 west a quarter mile. On the north end of town, turn west at the Dairy Queen, or drive north out of Chatfield on Route 52 about 2 miles to Spring Road SE, and go west to the narrow bridge. The creek has about five miles of fair fishing, but you may have to go upstream a bit to avoid the more heavily fished stretch at the edge of town. The creek is partially wooded upstream, but winds through open fields in its lower reaches. A portion of this creek just north of town has been improved.

Chatfield is a pretty town set in what is known locally as the "Chosen Valley." There are several gas stations here, a couple of convenience stores and a number of good cafes on the main street through town. Like a handful of other towns in the southeast, Chatfield throws an annual trout festival, celebrating its proximity to some very fine fishing.

Follow Route 52 south out of Chatfield, then turn east on Route 40 (formerly Rte. 103; still marked as such on the map). Lynch Creek flows under the bridge on Route 40 (map 2). Even early in the season, the creek may be dry under the bridge, but there are springs not far below this point, and the flow becomes steady to where it meets the Root River. This creek has a few miles of decent fishing but, since there's no direct access other than this bridge, you'll have to hike a few hundred yards downstream to it.

Continuing east on Route 40, you'll come to Route 30 at the old abandoned schoolhouse. If you keep going straight, you'll cross Route 30 and the road will turn to gravel. A little less than a mile down the gravel road, you'll come to Trout Run Creek at a three-culvert slab bridge.

Upstream from this bridge is a popular pasture stretch; downstream, a mix of woods and pasture. Both directions offer very good, if occasionally crowded, fishing. Try fishing here, or keep going until you come to a stop sign at a "T" in the road. The Pilot Mound cemetery will be on your right. Turn left (or north) and the next two gravel roads on the left, one a quarter mile and the next about a mile, will take you back to Trout Run, upstream from the slab bridge. The first left takes you to the bridge at a spot called "Bide-A-Wee." The second left winds down to the bridge at the now-famous round barn. The rickety old bridge below the barn has been replaced by a new, equally narrow concrete slab. Both these roads cross the stream and come out at a north-south road, which is Route 11 or Route 43, depending on which side of the Olmsted/Fillmore county line you're

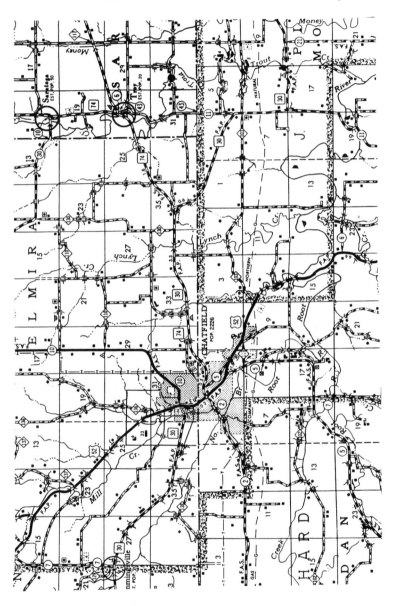

Map 2

standing (map 2). This road has been paved and moved slightly to the east since the first edition of this book. Although it changed the character of this quiet little valley, especially when road crews removed several dozen acres of oaks and other hardwoods, the road now can handle the heavy truck traffic that used to make parking along this stretch a little hairy. (This road – Route 11/43 – forms a shortcut from Route 30 to Route 74 north to the Interstate, saving the truckers about 8 miles of driving.) If you go north, you'll find the creek again where Route 43 (as it's marked here) crosses it and then parallels it all the way to the crossroads of Troy. There's good fishing all along the stream south of Troy, with a mix of meadow and wooded streamside. The stream is narrower here with fewer fish than at the three bridges downstream, but it's a nice place if you're looking to encounter fewer anglers. If you head south on Route 43/11, you'll meet up with Route 30 again, which makes a sharp curve to the east about a mile south of this junction. A mile after the curve, you'll come to the curiously named Bucksnort Dam on Trout Run. (The road sign at the bridge reads "Trout Creek.") Fishing is good above and below the old dam, and there is a small county park at the dam where you can leave your car.

Trout Run Creek is unquestionably one of the premier trout streams in the southeast. It tumbles through a beautiful, winding valley and offers more than a dozen miles of outstanding fishing from Troy to where it joins the Root River.

Go back west on Route 30 to Route 11 south (left at the big curve). Route 11 crosses the Root River and winds its way to the town of Fountain (map 3). Along the way, you'll notice a large number of sinkholes in the area, marked by circular clusters of trees growing out of depressions in the middle of corn fields and pasture land. These sinkholes are the result of the limestone topography of this region. They

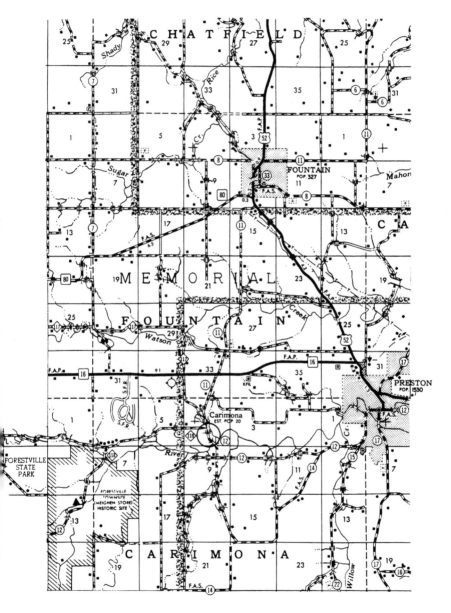

Map 3

funnel rain and snowmelt into a shallow aquifer and help feed the many springs that rise in the area around Fountain. No one in this pretty town has ever been able to tell me how the town got its name, but the word "fountain" was commonly used for "spring" well into the 20th century, and the headwaters of Rice Creek were once known locally as "Big Springs."

If you're interested in trying Rice Creek, take Route 8 west out of Fountain, then take the very first right onto the gravel road that goes past the quarry. Rice Creek rises in a small cave beside this narrow road and its flow is bolstered by a small valley of springs a little farther down, just above the sportsman's club pond. The creek is small here and you'll only find a mile or so of accessible water, most of it between the two bridges.

Go back to Fountain the way you came and take Route 11 south to Carimona. At Carimona, go west on Route 118, which runs parallel to the South Branch of the Root River, and will lead you into Forestville State Park (map 3). This is a beautiful park with excellent facilities. Many of the campsites are right beside the Root River. Access is excellent, although there's greater fishing pressure on this stretch of the river, particularly on weekends.

There are a couple of smaller creeks that join the South Branch of the Root River within the park. (Be sure to pick up a park map to help you find the creeks and trails.) South Branch Creek, called Canfield Creek on the park map, joins it near the primitive group camp. Like Rice Creek, Canfield Creek rises full-blown from the mouth of a cave, and it's worth the short hike to see the source even if the fishing here produces only small trout. North Branch Creek, called Forestville Creek on the park map, joins the Root near the picnic area. This creek is more productive than Canfield.

You'll want to stop at the Meighan Store, an 1850s stagecoach stop and general store abandoned around 1910, but perfectly preserved within the limits of the park.

This brings us to the end of the first section. If you are returning to Rochester, you can follow Route 118 out of the park to Route 12, then take Route 12 to Preston. Pick up Route 52 going north out of Preston and this will lead you back to Rochester.

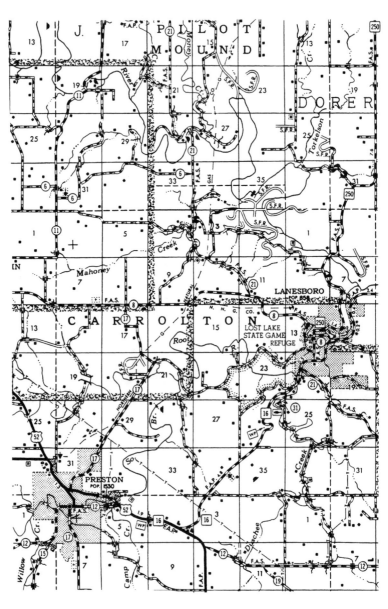

Map 4

AROUND LANESBORO

SOUTH BRANCH OF THE ROOT RIVER • WILLOW CREEK • CAMP CREEK • DUSCHEE CREEK • GRIBBEN CREEK • DIAMOND CREEK

From Forestville State Park, we travel east to the historic and beautiful town of Lanesboro. Between the park and the town, the South Branch of the Root River boasts more than twenty miles of good fishing. There are a number of crossings along Route 12, as well as access within the park and in the town of Lanesboro. Most significant is the new Root River State Trail, a ribbon of blacktop more than 35 miles long that follows the abandoned railroad grade from Fountain through Preston and Lanesboro and east to Rushford. It provides access for the angler on foot or bicycle. If you are looking to fish the Root River at its least-accessible stretches, consider taking a bike and a pack rod when you head for Lanesboro, then hop on the Root River State Trail as it passes through town. The trail crosses more than 45 bridges, some up to 500 feet long, providing unprecedented access to the Root River. (See Appendix for more information.)

As you drive from the park to Lanesboro, there are a number of small creeks that feed into the Root that you'll want to try along the way.

Go back to Carimona the way you came and follow Route 12 east toward Preston (map 4). Route 12 crosses Willow Creek just west of Preston. Though it flows beneath Route 12, you're better off heading south on Route 15 and going a mile and a half upstream to the bridge. The Willow is grazed to its banks and forded by cattle along much of its length between the bridges. But in the vicinity of the upstream bridge, it has better character (and good numbers of trout), and you will have lost nothing by trying this little creek.

Just east of the town of Preston, Route 12 crosses Camp Creek. Where it meets the Root here, Camp Creek is small, sluggish and uninviting. But further upstream it is an appealing meadow creek in a beautiful little valley. It has recently been improved by the DNR, which will increase its holding capacity and spawning areas for trout. It also has attracted the attention of anglers, who flock to it on opening day and in the first few weeks of the season.

To find the upper stretches, go into the pretty town of Preston (which bills itself as the "Trout Fishing Capital of Minnesota" and has its own "Trout Days" early in the season) on Route 12, then go south on St. Paul Street near the county courthouse. St. Paul descends to a bridge spanning the Root River, where it becomes Ridge Street. Follow Ridge to Cottage Grove Avenue on the left and go east on Cottage Grove. Somewhere up this little street lined with houses, Cottage Grove Avenue becomes Camp Creek Road. There are no road signs indicating this, but that's what the locals call it. Follow this road a mile or so to the bridge that crosses the creek. The improved section is downstream from here, but don't be afraid to explore the wooded stretch upstream.

If you continue east on Camp Creek Road, you'll hit Route 52. Go north on Route 52 to Route 16 and turn east again toward Lanesboro (map 4).

Just west of Lanesboro another small stream joins the Root. Duschee (commonly pronounced "dutchy") is a creek cursed by its own good fortune. It is a narrow meandering stream that flows clear and cold through a deep, steep-walled valley. It has been improved for much of its length and a narrow road runs the length of the lower stream, providing good access. But it also happens to be the location of the Lanesboro State Trout Hatchery, which was established in the 1920s by Thaddeus Surber (p. 77) on the site of an old mill near the mouth. The hatchery is the state's largest producer of trout. This undoubtedly leads many to assume that the stream is as good as it is, and fishing pressure here is fairly heavy. In addition, the DNR and Trout Unlimited continued stream improvement work during the 1997 season. But it is, despite these pressures, a small stream of particular charm, challenge and quality, and worth a visit.

To access Duschee Creek, take Route 16 east from Preston toward Lanesboro and turn south on Route 31 a mile past the wayside park. Route 31 is well marked as the site of the trout hatchery, so follow the signs and continue upstream past the hatchery to gain access to more than seven miles of fishing.

Go back to Route 16 the way you came and continue east into Lanesboro. This is unquestionably among the most scenic towns in Minnesota. *Outside* Magazine even called it one of the "best places" in America, and land prices have been soaring there in recent years. Much of the town is built on a high limestone rampart in the middle of a big bend in the Root River and the entire business district is on the National Register of Historic Places. The town has much to offer the angler and the tourist: there's excellent fishing on the Root River as it sweeps through town, there are some fine little cafes and many excellent bed-and-breakfasts in the rolling countryside surrounding the town. There's also a nice park on the main street below the dam, where you can have a picnic or watch the children fish for trout in the stocked pond.

East of Lanesboro, just past the town of Whalan, two small creeks join the Root River. Gribben Creek (Marked "Gribb" on the county maps) and Diamond Creek offer limited fishing. Gribben is a very small, brushy creek, but roughly 3 miles of the creek have been improved by the DNR. Go east on Route 16 to Route 23 south. Park at this crossing and work your way upstream. By mid- to late summer, the banks are often too overgrown to allow you do much more than dap this tiny creek.

Diamond Creek has also been improved upstream in the state forest land. Take Route 16 about a mile and a half east of Gribben Creek to a minimum-maintenance road to the right. Go upstream past the posted lands and the old schoolhouse. The creek is very small, but supports a healthy population of wild trout.

Go back to Lanesboro the way you came. If you are returning to Rochester, simply retrace your steps along Route 16 west to Route 52 and head north.

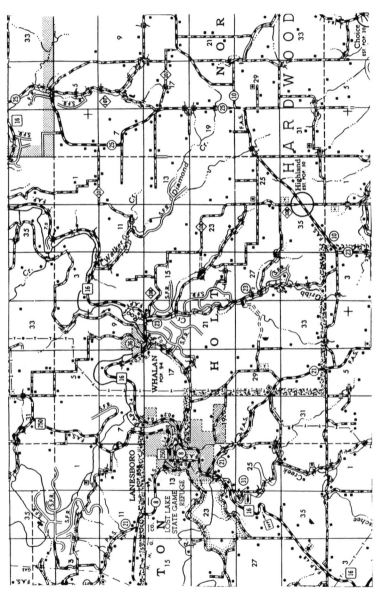

Map 5

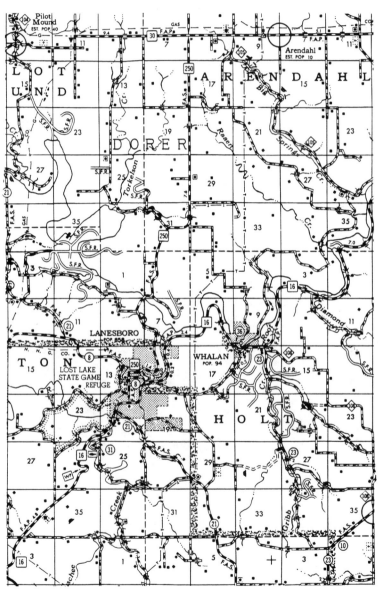

Map 6

EAST TO RUSHFORD

TORKELSON CREEK • BIG SPRINGS CREEK • PINE
CREEK (FREMONT TOWNSHIP) • COOLRIDGE CREEK •
HEMMINGWAY CREEK • RUSH CREEK

The next section takes us from Lanesboro to the town of Rushford. We'll visit a half dozen creeks in some of the prettiest scenery you'll find in the state. Thaddeus Surber, in his 1924 report to the Game and Fish Commissioner, described the area this way:

> "The deepest and narrowest gorges on the lower valley [of the Root River] are found between Whalan and Peterson; here the valley becomes so narrow in places the entire bottom-lands hardly provide room for the railroad beside the water-course; along here it is picturesque in the extreme, and it is doubtful if some of the scenery here can be equaled, most certainly not excelled, by any other section of the state. As an example take the bluffs at Rushford with their rugged barren faces rising to an altitude of 565 feet above the river."

Surber spent two full years following every mile of the Root River and its tributaries, on foot and on horseback. His

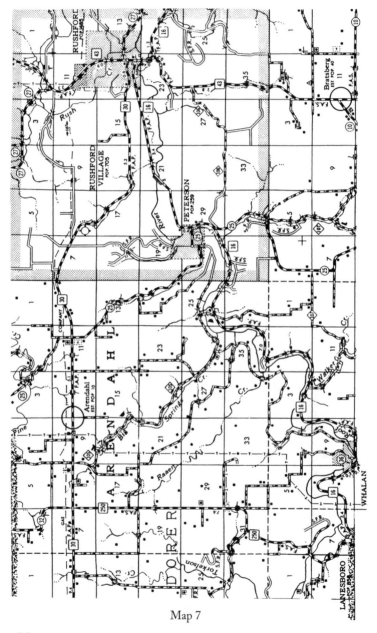

Map 7

report, now a collector's item, details each tributary and its potential as a trout stream. Anyone nostalgic for the "good old days" would be surprised at how few trout Surber found in southeastern Minnesota in the years following World War I. He reported that poaching took a huge toll on what trout populations there were, and the heavy erosion due to logging and grazing created so much roily water that the Root River resembled, as he put it, "the 'Big Muddy' in general appearance."

Though much has changed since Surber's expedition, I'd like to think he'd still recognize this stretch of the Root River, and find it and its tributaries in much better condition.

The first creek we'll visit on this leg of our trip is a very small creek that flows into the North Branch of the Root just north of Lanesboro. If you like the challenge of small streams, you'll want to visit Torkelson Creek. To find it, follow Route 250 north across the South Branch of the Root and out of Lanesboro (map 6). This road crosses the North Branch at an old iron bridge after a mile or so, then climbs out of the valley. (Don't be afraid to fish the North Branch here. In early season, I have cast to large trout in this broad stretch of water.) Just past the green mile marker 5, Route 250 makes a swing to the east. At this curve, a small gravel lane goes off to the left, or northwest. Follow this road (it has no number) as it winds down through a very narrow and beautiful valley. After about a mile the road parallels a nameless creek and you will come to the North Branch again. Here you will cross Torkelson Creek. Park here and follow this creek upstream to where it has been improved, and a couple of springs boost the flow. And if you catch a few of the trout that are here, you'll be even more pleased to know that Surber classified this challenging little stream as "unfit for restocking."

Return to Route 250 the way you came and continue north until you meet Route 30. Go east on Route 30 about a mile to Route 105 south. This winding road leads all the way to the town of Peterson, following Big Springs Creek for much of the way. Big Springs is aptly named, as large springs form broad, cold pools along the east side of the road. These large springs flow under the road to join the creek, which is very narrow, flowing along the west side of the road. You'll find a mile or so, at best, of good trout water here, but the springs are unique and interesting.

The road swings east when it meets the Root, and will lead you into the town of Peterson. This town was settled by a man by the name of (what else?) Peterson, who is credited with creating the first trout hatchery in the state.

The Root River State Trail runs through town along the old railroad grade on its way from Lanesboro to Rushford.

Follow Route 25 north out of Peterson (Map 8). Route 25 becomes Route 29 at the Winona/Fillmore county line. Just before the county line, you'll cross Pine Creek. A small minimum-maintenance road goes east just before this bridge. Follow this gravel road to where it peters out at the creek and fish upstream or down from here – but mind the posted signs and, when in doubt, ask permission.

Continue north on 29 to Route 2, then turn east to Coolridge Creek. Follow Route 2 across Coolridge to where it joins Pine Creek. A mile or so east of this junction, a narrow lane goes south, or right, to a small bridge and a fisherman's parking lot. This section of Pine Creek has been improved and shows great promise, although most of the trout I've caught here recently were stocked fish. It will take a few seasons for the improved section to begin to produce wild fish.

Walk upstream about a mile and a half to where Hemmingway Creek flows into the Pine. Hemmingway was known for years as one of the finest little brook-trout creeks

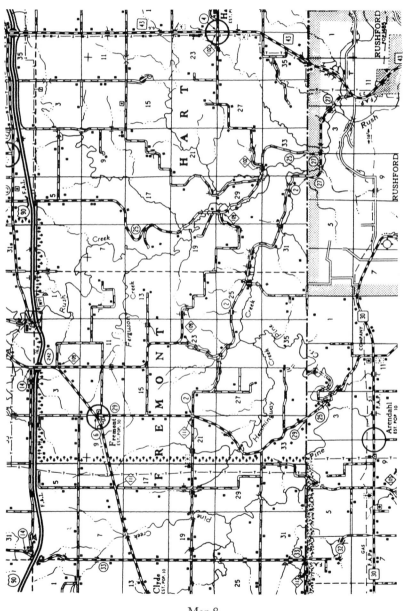

Map 8

in the region. Heavy fishing pressure and a few years of drought took a toll on this pretty little creek, but it is certainly worth exploring, and Pine Creek has always been a good off-the-beaten-path stream.

Continue southeast on Route 2 to the county line where it becomes 27. Just over the county line, Route 27 crosses Rush Creek (map 9). Turn north, or left, just past this bridge, and follow the recently upgraded Route 25 as it parallels Rush Creek. This outstanding creek has been improved by the DNR and boasts more than a dozen miles of fair to good fishing. The problem lies in gaining access. There are only a couple of bridges that cross the creek and they're not much help; the creekbed is silted and difficult to wade, and the streambanks overhung with vegetation. Your best bet is to seek out the landowners to obtain permission to cross their land to the better water.

Go back south on Route 25 to Route 27, then south to where it meets Route 43. Take Route 43 south to the town of Rushford. This town offers plenty of services for the traveler. If you're returning to Rochester, simply follow Route 43 north to I90, and go west to Rochester.

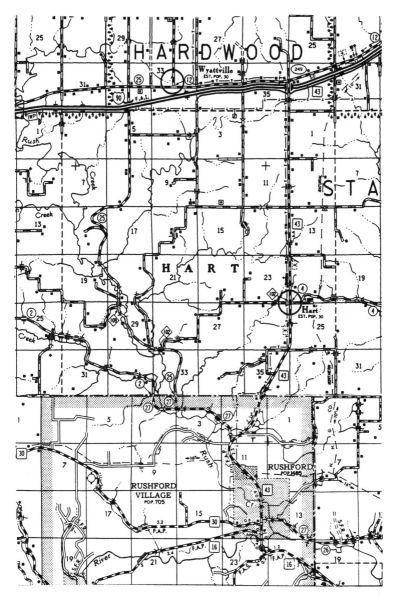

Map 9

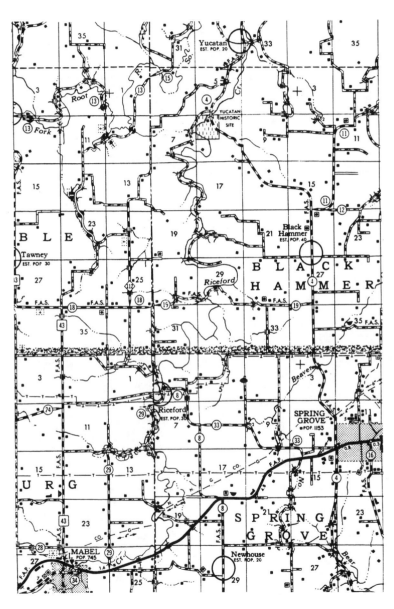

Map 10

SOUTH OF RUSHFORD

MAPLE CREEK • SOUTH FORK OF THE ROOT RIVER •
NEPSTAD CREEK • WISEL CREEK •
RICEFORD CREEK • BEE CREEK (WATERLOO CREEK) •
EAST BEAVER CREEK • WEST BEAVER CREEK

At a broad bend in the Riceford Creek, not far from the fork in the road called "Yucatan," (map 10, opposite) lie the remains of more than two dozen Native Americans. Discovered during road-widening construction in the early 1940s, the graves were excavated by a team of archaeologists from the University of Minnesota. After the excavation and initial analysis, however, the 300-year-old bones lay mostly forgotten in cardboard boxes in the basement of a building on the Minneapolis campus. In 1982, I had the opportunity to be part of a team that studied the skeletons for the first time in decades. Puzzled by a consistent bone deformity common to nearly all 27 individuals, I drove down to the excavation site – a place in the southeast I'd never been – just to see where these people had lived, died and been buried. I was so struck by the beauty and solitude of the site, I've returned to it every year for the last decade and a half.

Before our labwork could be completed, the Native American community requested that the skeletons and their

85

associated artifacts be reburied. One of the skeletons, identi-fied as the remains of a teenage boy, was reburied with an item that must have been very important to him: a small bone fishhook.

A short time after the reburials, I stopped by Tom Helgeson's old fly shop and bumped into a man who'd been a part of the excavation team almost 50 years earlier. I was not surprised to learn that he was an avid trout fisherman; it was this quiet bend on the Riceford Creek that reinforced my love for the places where trout live and became the cata-lyst for this book.

Most of the streams between Rushford and the Iowa border flow north into the South Fork of the Root River. Here the villages have evocative names like Choice, Prosper and Harmony. There's a large Amish community in the sur-rounding area, and their horse-drawn carriages are a com-mon sight. The rivers too seem to evoke an earlier time. If you're looking to escape the more crowded streams, this handful of creeks may be your ticket.

You can reach Rushford by following I90 east out of Rochester to Highway 43 south at exit 249. Take 43 all the way into Rushford. Continue south out of Rushford on Route 43. About 10 miles south of town you'll come to the unmarked Maple Creek (map 11). This little brook-trout creek runs through private land for most of its length, but is worth a short detour.

Continue south on 43 to the settlement of Choice. Here, the South Fork of the Root flows through a beautiful valley with picturesque limestone ramparts. Work your way upstream (it's sluggish and silty downstream). Nepstad Creek joins it a mile upstream, and is a stream worth visit-ing as well.

Or, continue south on Route 43 to Route 12. Turn right on 12 and go west until you cross the South Fork again at the new bridge. Fish upstream or down from this bridge.

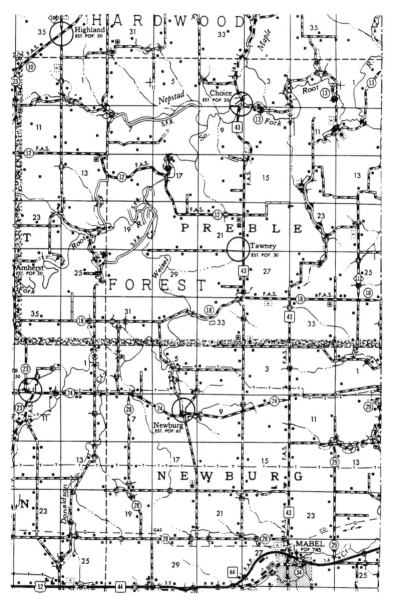

Map 11

Continue west on 12 about a mile or so to the first gravel road on the left, marked "Minimum Maintenance Road." Follow this tiny lane south to a "T" in the road, then turn left to a small bridge over the South Fork. At this point the creek is very small, but it holds trout, especially in the warmer months as the trout seek cooler water near the springs.

Halfway between this bridge and the one downstream, Wisel Creek (spelled "Weisel" on the county map) flows into the South Fork from the south. This confluence usually fishes well and can be reached by hiking down from here, or by continuing south on the gravel road to Route 18. Turn east, or left, on 18 and follow it until you come to the bridge over Wisel Creek. This little stream flows sluggishly under the bridge, which is a popular spot for spin- and bait fishermen. But upstream it flows a little more quickly through a mix of woodland and meadow (and, unfortunately, an old garbage dump). Work your way downstream to the confluence with the South Fork of the Root. Like many of the little streams of the southeast, Wisel has a great deal of potential, and could become a truly great trout creek with some stream-improvement work.

Continue east on Route 18 until it joins Route 43. Follow 43 south toward the town of Mabel. Three miles south of 18, turn east on the gravel road. This road goes past the Sportsman's Park, with its old mill pond and tough-to-catch rainbows, then crosses the Riceford Creek. The creek here is small. You can fish here or follow the road north to the old crossroads of Riceford. An iron bridge crosses the creek near a cluster of interesting old buildings. Downstream for several miles the creek is slow and fairly infertile, but it's popular with anglers from the surrounding area, and produces some good stocked-trout carryover from season to season. The Riceford is another creek that would clearly improve with stream work. It has good, steady flow, although flashy in storms, and flows through a very beautiful valley.

To reach the lower stretches of Riceford Creek, take

Route 8 to Route 33 to Spring Grove. Turn north on Route 4 to the crossroads of Black Hammer with its historic general store. Turn left, or west, and follow this winding road to where it meets the creek again, and follow the road north to where it rejoins Route 4. You can continue north on 4 to Route 76 which goes north to the town of Houston or south to Caledonia; or take Route 4 south, back to Spring Grove. In this pretty little town you'll find several gas stations, and ample places to eat or stay the night.

Just south of Spring Grove, Bee Creek flows south roughly parallel to Route 27 through the settlement of Bee and into Iowa, where it becomes Waterloo Creek (map 12). (The DeLorme and DOT maps call it Waterloo Creek on the Minnesota side of the state line.) Bee Creek benefits from the put-and-take stocking program south of the border. Hold-over trout find their way into the Minnesota portion of the creek and make this small stream a worthwhile stop. In fact, if you're heading for Bee Creek, buy an Iowa license, too. You won't want to miss any of this creek. (For more information on Waterloo Creek, pick up a copy of *Iowa Trout Streams*, by Jene Hughes.) To reach Bee, follow the winding Route 27 south from the east side of Spring Grove a couple of miles and turn right on either of the first two gravel roads on the right. The first gravel road takes you past an old quarry and into Bee. If you take the first gravel road, bear left at the "T" in the road; if you take the second gravel road, bear right at the "T". Both of these roads lead to Bee Creek just north of the border. (Or, if you prefer, Route 16 south out of Spring Grove will take you directly to Waterloo Creek at Dorchester, Iowa. Simply follow the creek upstream to the state line at Bee.)

Return to Spring Grove the way you came, or continue south into Iowa to the town of Dorchester on Route A16. Just past Dorchester, take Route 76 north to the state line and all the way to Caledonia.

If you're planning to camp and fish south of Rushford, Beaver Creek Valley State Park just west of Caledonia is a great place to combine the two. My father and I fished together all over the U.S. and Canada, but I count our overnight camping and fishing trips to Beaver Creek Valley among the best and most relaxing. We could leave work in the Twin Cities at noon, stop for lunch along the road and have camp set up by four o'clock. Then we'd fish until dark, fix dinner and sit in folding chairs next to a campfire and watch the sparks from the fire mingle with the bright stars overhead as we talked. At dawn the next day, we'd be on the water, sometimes startling a few deer, and fish until it was time for breakfast. After breakfast, we'd pack up camp and head back to the Cities where we'd be back at work by one o'clock. A single day off that felt like three.

To find Beaver Creek Valley State Park (map 13), follow Route 76 west out of Caledonia to Route 1 and watch for the signs.

Deep in the park, East Beaver Creek rises from a bubbling spring at the base of a 300-foot limestone cliff near the camping area. The spring produces a high volume of water, which runs clear as gin to where it meets West Beaver Creek in the northwest corner of the park.

The park itself is one of the prettiest and most intimate in the state. It offers a variety of campsites, and to reach them you must drive through the stream itself. There are plenty of hiking trails along the creek and atop the bluffs. There is also a historic mill, Schech's Mill, just north of the park on Route 10. It is open for tours during the season.

West Beaver Creek is a small, brook-trout stream that is paralleled by Route 12 most of its length. To reach West Beaver Creek, return to Route 76 and turn north 1 mile to Route 10. Turn west on 10 and follow it to the iron bridge across the Beaver near Schech's Mill. Take the first left after the bridge and go south. About a mile down the road, a small dirt lane goes off to the left and will lead you to the

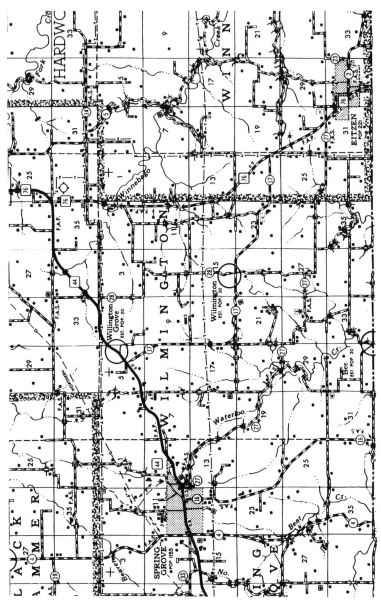

Map 12

Beaver in the northwest corner of the park. You can park here and follow the stream, or continue south on the main road to where it crosses the West Beaver at a couple of small bridges on Route 12.

To return to Rochester from here, return to Route 10 the way you came, and follow 10 north along Beaver Creek to where 10 meets Route 76. Follow 76 north through Houston; it will take you all the way to I90. Take I90 west to Rochester.

If you are returning to Rochester from Spring Grove or Caledonia, you can follow Route 44 east to where it joins Route 52, and follow 52 all the way back to Rochester.

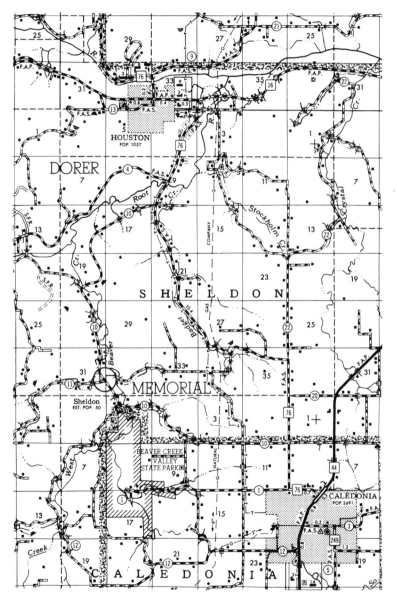

Map 13

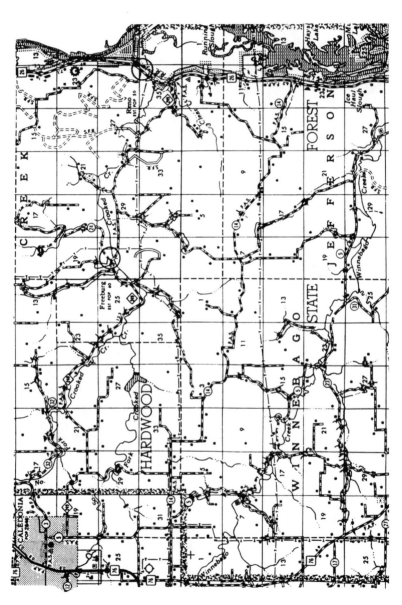

Map 14

SOUTHEAST OF CALEDONIA

NORTH FORK CROOKED CREEK • SOUTH FORK CROOKED CREEK • WINNEBAGO CREEK

Here in this quiet corner of the state, only a handful of miles from Iowa and Wisconsin, are a couple of overlooked and underrated streams that are worth a visit: Crooked Creek and Winnebago Creek.

Both are tributaries of the Mississippi River and flow roughly west to east through broad, shallow valleys more reminiscent of those of the "Coulee" region just across the river in Wisconsin.

To reach Crooked Creek (map 14), take Main Street east from Route 76/44 in Caledonia. Main Street is Route 249, which turns south at North Winnebago Street, then east again south of town. Route 249 will take you across the North Fork of Crooked Creek. The South Fork joins the North about three miles downstream from the first bridge.

Follow 249 all the way to the town of Freeburg. There are several places between the first bridge on 249 and Freeburg where you can get access to this narrow, but productive, creek. It is thin water in places, posted in others, and grazed more than I think it ought to be, but it is a fine little stream with several miles of good fishing.

Return to Caledonia on Route 249 the way you came. Route 5 goes south from Caledonia where Route 249 turns north at N. Winnebago Street. Follow 5 south all the way to where it meets Winnebago Creek (map 15). Route 5 parallels the creek practically its entire length.

Although there are some posted sections along the creek's lower stretches, access is better than what you may have read; and for the angler willing to walk, there are literally miles of fine fishing along this quiet stream.

These streams may not justify a trip from Minneapolis, Madison or Chicago, but if you're in the area, make the short detour; I recommend them both.

Return to Caledonia the way you came. If you're returning to Rochester, take 76 north to I90 and go west. Or, take 44 east to 52 and head north.

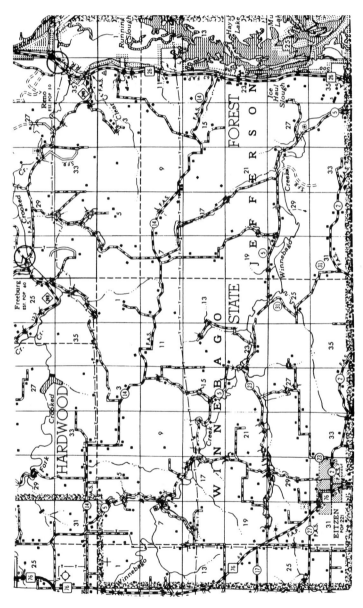

Map 15

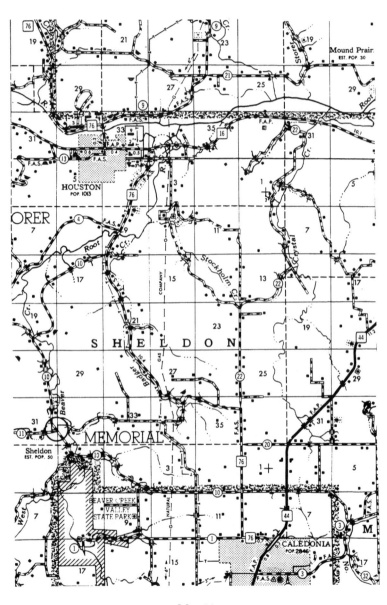

Map 16

NORTH TO PICKWICK

BADGER CREEK • LOONEY CREEK • SILVER CREEK •
PINE CREEK (NEW HARTFORD TOWNSHIP) •
PICKWICK CREEK (BIG TROUT CREEK) •
LITTLE PICKWICK CREEK (LITTLE TROUT CREEK)

From Caledonia we drive north to the town of Pickwick, and the nearby Great River Bluffs State Park (formerly O. L. Kipp State Park). As we travel north, we will leave the Root River watershed and conclude this section with a visit to a handful of small streams that flow directly into the Mississippi River.

Just south of Pickwick, Great River Bluffs State Park occupies a site on the high bluffs overlooking the Mississippi. The park, which offers good facilities for campers or picnickers, is well situated for exploring the area between Lacrosse, Wisconsin and Winona, Minnesota. Along here, the Mississippi is wide, sluggish and punctuated with sloughs and islands; the high bluffs dotted with fine apple orchards; and small creeks flow through crooked valleys into the big river.

These small creeks have a different character than the tributaries of the Root. They are less fertile and, in most cases, much narrower than the creeks to the west. They tend to be flashier in storms, carrying large volumes of water down their steep, narrow grades during heavy rains. But looks can be deceiving, and personal experience has taught me that these creeks can hold good trout populations.

Follow Route 76 north out of Caledonia toward the town of Houston (map 16). Route 76 meets Badger Creek about 7 miles north of Caledonia. The fishing is fair along this creek, with access at the bridge a couple of miles downstream.

From the town of Houston, take Route 76 to Route 9, which is the first right after you cross the broad concrete bridge spanning the Root River north of town. Interestingly, Route 76 used to link up directly with Route 9 and cross the river via an iron bridge a mile east of this new bridge. Many of the old maps still show this link, indicating a road where there's now only cornfield. The previous version of the DNR's "Trout Streams of Southeast Minnesota" map (the one with red lines indicating trout streams, rather than the current blue) showed this connection, confusing many fishermen including myself. As you make the turn onto Route 9, look off to the south across the fields and you'll see that the old iron bridge still stands, a picturesque relic in the middle of a cornfield.

Five miles up Route 9, the road crosses Silver Creek. This small creek, though a designated trout stream, has not been improved. Its shoreline is private and primarily overgrazed. Access is tough, as well, but it hardly matters as the fishing is virtually nonexistent. Looney Creek, which flows into Silver at the next bridge, is even worse. The broad Lunay valley, from which Looney Creek gets its name, seems to promise bigger streams, but it does not deliver.

Continue north along Route 9. This becomes Route 11 at the Winona county line just a mile or so farther north. Follow Route 11 to the head of the valley. Turn left on 11, then take the first right on Route 2. This gravel lane is a short cut to Route 8. Go east on 8 to Route 5. The map calls

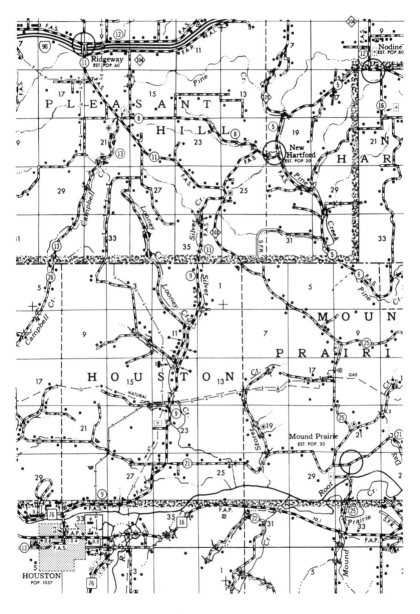

Map 17

101

this intersection "New Hartford," and it is also the place where the South Fork of Pine Creek meets Pine Creek. Pine is a small, silty creek that is prone to flashiness. It's not a very productive creek, but there are a couple of access points, including the old road right-of-way just south of New Hartford on 5.

Continue northeast on Route 5 to the town of Nodine, and turn north on Route 12, which crosses Interstate 90 about a mile up the road. Immediately north of I90, take Route 3 east, or right. This road is also called Apple Blossom Drive, a road deservedly designated "scenic" by the state legislature. Less than a mile east on this road you'll come to the entrance to the state park.

Just past the park on 3, take the first road on the left. Marked "Little Trout Valley," this small lane follows Little Pickwick Creek (also and aptly called Little Trout Creek) into the town of Pickwick. The middle stretches of this creek have been improved by the Win-Cres Chapter of Trout Unlimited. Look for the stiles over the fences. The creek is narrow enough to step across, but it offers several miles of good fishing in a quiet valley.

Continue down the valley to the town of Pickwick. There's a beautiful old mill in town that's open for tours, and a large mill pond just above it. The pond, an impound-ment of Pickwick Creek (or Big Trout Creek), is itself desig-nated trout water.

Route 7 goes south out of town, following Pickwick Creek upstream. Pickwick Creek has several miles of decent fishing with good access. Look for a narrow lane marked Route 6 that goes off to the east. There's a small bridge across the creek and a stile to allow you to cross the fence. This creek, though small, has a unique and appealing char-acter, and is definitely worth exploring.

If you follow Route 7 up the valley, you'll come to Route 12 at I90 again. Turn east and follow this road back to Route 3 and the state park. Or, if you are returning to Rochester, access I90 at the bridge and go west.

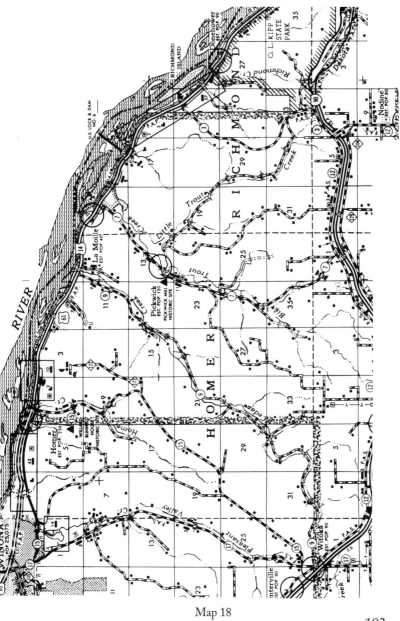

Map 18

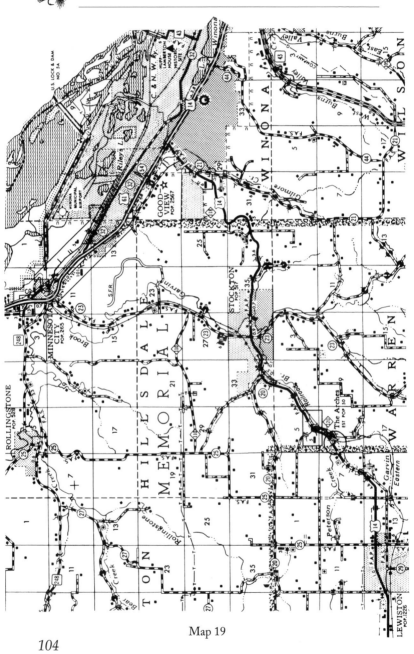

Map 19

Northwest toward Rollingstone

Cedar Valley Creek • Pleasant Valley Creek •
East Burns Valley Creek • Gilmore Creek •
Garvin Brook • Stockton Valley Creek •
Rupprecht Creek (Rollingstone Creek) •
Bear Creek

The next trip takes us from Great River Bluffs State Park to Whitewater State Park, and a handful of creeks in between. The character of these creeks is similar to Pickwick: small streams rushing through deep, narrow valleys. The geography of the area makes getting from one stream to the next a rather long trip, as one must drive the full length of the first valley to get to the next. Here the remoteness of the Root River valley is replaced by greater population density. These narrow valleys empty into the vast Mississippi near the city of Winona, which in turn is slowly pouring development into the valleys. This can occasionally give the angler the feeling of fishing in a subdivision.

Traveling west from the state park, follow the road down Little Trout Valley into Pickwick again. Turn right, or northeast, on Route 7 and you'll come to Highway 61 in a couple of miles. Turn left, or northwest, on 61 and then left again, or southeast, on route 9 at the town of La Moille. Route 9 parallels Cedar Valley Creek through its entire length. The road crosses the creek several times and access is generally good. Fishing can be decent, but mind the golf balls from the 18-hole course that parallels the creek on the opposite side of the creek.

Follow 9 to the head of the valley and continue into the town of Witoka. At Witoka, turn north again on Route 17 toward Winona and you will plunge into Pleasant Valley. Pleasant Valley Creek is even smaller than Cedar, and here development changes the character of the fishing, particularly in the lower stretches.

Continue down Route 17 to just before Highway 61. Here you have a choice: you can take Route 105 south along East Burns Valley Creek, though the fishing is at best spotty; or you can follow 61 northeast to Route 14 and Gilmore Creek. This little creek is usually more promising than Burns Valley, though it too is fairly developed. Route 21 parallels the creek up the narrow valley.

Go back to Route 14 and turn west toward the town of Stockton. The two creeks of Garvin Brook and Stockton Valley Creek converge at Stockton and flow into the Mississippi at Minnesota City. During the summer of 1991, while I was preparing the first edition of this book, a heavy storm turned these two fine trout streams into a single rushing torrent and devastated much of the area. Today there is little evidence of the flood, other than some newer housing developments built for Stockton residents who lost their homes to the flood waters. The fishing has returned, though the streams seem more silted than I remember them.

Route 23 follows Stockton Valley Creek upstream, while Route 14 parallels Garvin Brook and the lovely winding railroad grade and stone bridges through the town of The Arches, at the head of the valley.

Go back to Stockton the way you came, and turn north on Route 27. Follow 27 to Route 110, which goes west about a mile north of town. Follow Route 110 to Route 25 and turn north on 25 toward the town of Rollingstone. Turn west on Route 248 at Rollingstone and you will cross Rupprecht Creek, also known as Rollingstone Creek. Turn south on Route 27, which crosses Bear Creek a half mile above its junction with Rupprecht Creek. Rupprecht offers several miles of good fishing in this pretty valley, but access may be hard to come by. Bear Creek is not as good.

Go back to Route 248 and turn west toward the town of Altura. From here we enter the Whitewater River watershed, and some of the most popular trout fishing in the southeast, if not the best. If you are returning to Rochester, take Route 33 south to Route 14 west, which will take you back to the city.

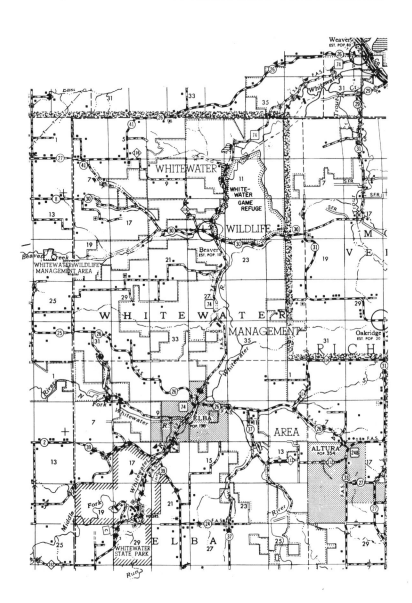

Map 20

West to the Whitewater Branches

North, Middle & South Branches of the
Whitewater River • Trout Run Creek •
Beaver Creek • Trout Valley Creek

The character and quality of the Whitewater River and its branches, combined with its proximity to Rochester and the Twin Cities, and its excellent facilities, make this area extremely popular. Even in winter, when special regulations allow catch-and-release trout fishing on several of the branches, it is not uncommon to find an angler every few hundred yards along the river.

A large portion of the nearly 300 square miles that make up the Whitewater watershed is public land. As a result, the river bottoms and the surrounding hills are home to a diverse variety of wildlife, including deer, wild turkey and grouse, all of which can be hunted here in season.

The Whitewater watershed is made up of three forks or branches: the North, Middle and South, with several smaller tributaries, including Trout Run Creek, Beaver Creek and Trout Valley Creek all joining it along the way.

Within this watershed are two state parks, Whitewater State Park straddling the Middle Fork of the Whitewater, and Carley State Park on the North Fork. Both parks offer camping, hiking and picnicking facilities, as well as the trout fishing, in spectacular scenery.

Whitewater State Park, the larger of the two parks, offers excellent camping facilities, but is often crowded. You'd be wise to call ahead (see Appendix) if you plan to camp.

From the town of Altura, where the last chapter left off, follow Route 26 west to the little town of Elba just north of the park (map 20). Turn south on Route 74 through town and this will lead you to the park. It's a good idea to pick up a park map, which will show you the trails along the river. Fishing pressure within the park can be heavy, but the fishing is usually pretty good. The short, but scenic, Trout Run Creek (not to be confused with the one near Chatfield) joins the Middle Branch (or "Middle Fork") near the park's south picnic area. Trout Run has only a few pools, but it contains good numbers of trout, including rainbows.

The Middle Branch flows through the park to the town of Elba, where it is joined by the North Branch. There are several places within the park to access the Middle Branch. South of the park, you can access its upper stretches by driving south on Route 74 to Route 152 or Route 9. Go west on either of these to the bridges.

Return to the park the way you came and follow Route

74 into Elba. Turn west on Fairwater Drive, just past the Mauer Brother's Tavern, and you'll follow the North Branch for a mile or so. Hike upstream to find good fishing.

Go back to Elba and turn east on Route 26. The second bridge you hit crosses the South Branch of the Whitewater. You can park at this popular spot and fish upstream or down, or take Route 26 east to Route 37 and turn right, or south, and follow 37 along the South Branch (or "South Fork") of the Whitewater. There's good fishing all along here. Continue south on 37 to Route 112. Turn east on 112 to the new walking bridge, which was built since the first edition of this book to replace the old abandoned automobile bridge. This is a good spot to park and walk upstream. The South Branch is one of the finest streams in the southeast, although it gets quite a bit of pressure, and the hike upstream is worth the trip.

To reach the upper stretches of the South Branch by car, go back to Route 26 and turn right, or east, and follow it into Altura. Turn right on 248 into town, then turn right again and follow Route 112 down a narrow valley until you find the South Branch again. Turn left and follow this two-track along the creek until you come to a cattle gate. The farmer allows some camping and fishing here, but be sure to close the gate behind you.

Return to Elba the way you came. The Main Branch of the Whitewater flows north along Route 74 and into the Mississippi at the town of Weaver. Beaver Creek joins the Main Branch at the old Beaver townsite, now just a cross-roads of Routes 74 and 30. Route 30 east follows Beaver Creek for about a mile. There's a state park limited-access road that goes south from Route 30 just before 30 veers away from the creek. Park here and work your way upstream or down. Beaver Creek is full of trout, but it is heavily overgrown and excruciatingly tough to fish. I recommend it.

North of the crossroads of 30 and 74, Route 74 turns to gravel and the river gains width and depth, meandering through hundreds of acres of wildlife management area known as the Weaver Bottoms. The character of the Whitewater changes as it nears the Mississippi, but it continues to support trout.

Just before Highway 61, Trout Valley Creek (marked "Trout Creek" on the county map, opposite) flows into the Whitewater from the south. This creek is sandy and infertile, but access is fairly good and the persistent angler will find a few trout. Turn south on Highway 61 and then west again on Route 29. At the first sharp turn, a small lane goes straight down to a bridge across the creek. Another crossing, a mile or so south on 29, looks more promising, although the creek is silted up from heavy grazing erosion upstream from here.

Return to the park the way you came or continue north on 61 to the next group of streams. If you are returning to Rochester, follow 61 south to Highway 14 west at Winona, or follow 74 south to Highway 14 at St. Charles and head west.

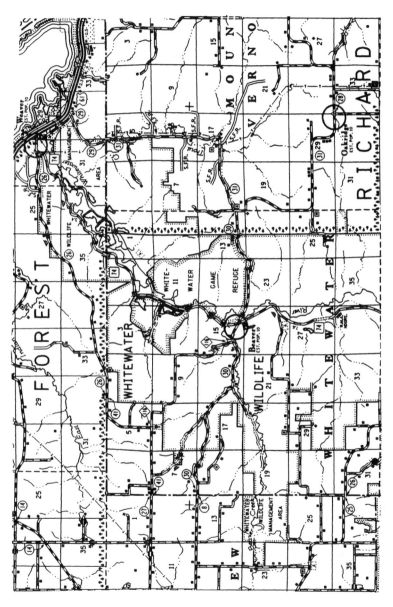

Map 21

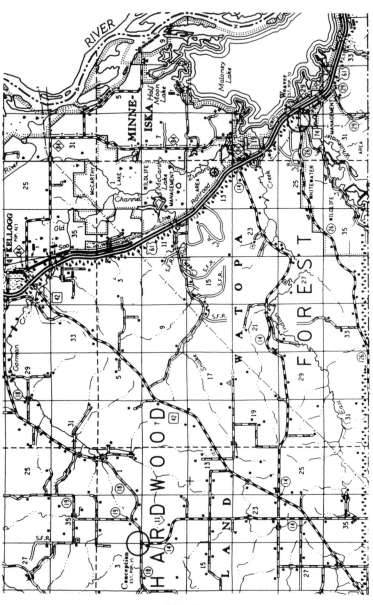

Map 22

North of Rochester

East Indian Creek • West Indian Creek •
Spring Creek • Cold Spring Creek •
Mazeppa Creek • Hay Creek

For a surprising number of Twin Cities-based trout anglers, an occasional trip to the streams between Rochester and Red Wing is their only experience with the southeast. Although there are only a handful of streams here, their proximity to the Twin Cities makes them an easy day trip or an evening's escape.

Unlike the streams in the Root or Whitewater watersheds, the northern creeks are few and widely scattered. If one of these streams is not fishing well, it's a longer drive to the nearest alternative.

Of these streams, the most popular by far (and by many accounts the most popular in the southeast) is Hay Creek.

Rising in springs a few miles north of Goodhue, it winds its way to the Mississippi River at the city of Red Wing. Hay Creek has undergone substantial stream-improvement work over the last decade. (Tragically, Hay Creek was the victim of an apparently intentional fish kill in July of 1997 that wiped out thousands of trout in the catch-and-release section of the stream. Although trout have already returned to this portion of the creek, it will be several seasons before the trout population in this stretch returns to its high pre-kill numbers.)

Whether you live in the Twin Cities, the Rochester area, or are just passing through, plan to spend some time on these northern streams.

If you're looking to camp in this area, there's an excellent state park just south of Red Wing on Highway 61. Frontenac State Park, like Great River Bluffs, stands on a high promontory above the Mississippi River and offers good camping or day-use facilities with commanding views of the Mississippi at Lake Pepin.

We continue our journey following Route 74 north from Whitewater State Park. Scarcely two miles north of the mouth of the Whitewater River another, smaller, creek flows into the Mississippi. East Indian Creek (map 22) is a fine little brook-trout creek with a mix of wooded and open streamside. Its most redeeming feature, however, is its lack of bridges. Route 14 parallels the stream at a safe distance for several miles, but does not cross it. Fortunately, there are easements and many of the landowners will allow you to cross their land – if you ask first. The DNR and TU are currently improving part of the stream, as well. It suffers from the same silty character as many of the small streams that flow directly into the Mississippi.

To find East Indian Creek, take Route 74 north from Whitewater to Highway 61 at Weaver. Take 61 north for a couple of miles to Route 14, and go west.

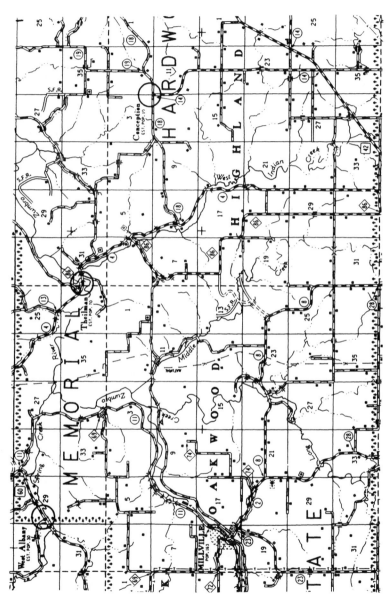

Map 23

West of East Indian Creek is the aptly named West
Indian Creek (map 23). Other than the name, however, the
twins have little else in common. West Indian is better
known as a brown-trout creek, is a tributary of the Zumbro
River, and has several bridges providing almost unlimited
access. As a result, West Indian receives fairly heavy fishing
pressure, particularly early in the season.

To find West Indian, continue west on Route 14, which
jogs north just past Route 42, and follow it to where it meets
Route 18. Go west on 18 until you meet the creek at Route 4.
Route 4 parallels West Indian for about six miles.

If you go south, or left, from here, you'll cross West
Indian at a newer concrete bridge. The vestiges of the old
bridge are just upstream of the new one, and this is a popular spot to fish. The creek has been improved upstream from
here, near the cinderblock compound of the sportsman's
club. Unfortunately, beavers are rapidly undoing much of
the improvement work.

About two miles north of the junction of Routes 4 and
18, Route 86 goes west and crosses the creek near the
Whippoorwill Campground. Fish upstream or down from
here. Or, continue north on 4, which crosses the creek once
more near the confluence with the Zumbro just south of the
town of Theilman.

Local anglers work the lower portions of the creek from
pool to pool, spending little time on the long stretches of
empty water in between.

Continue north on Route 4 to Route 60 and turn left, or
west. A few miles west on 60 you'll cross Spring Creek. This
small, marginal creek is best passed up in favor of the two
creeks farther west. The first, Cold Spring Brook, (marked
"Cold Creek" on the county map, opposite) has only a few
hundred yards of fishable water at best, but don't let that
discourage you. Cold Spring has an excellent trout population – including plenty of brookies – and is definitely worth
a visit.

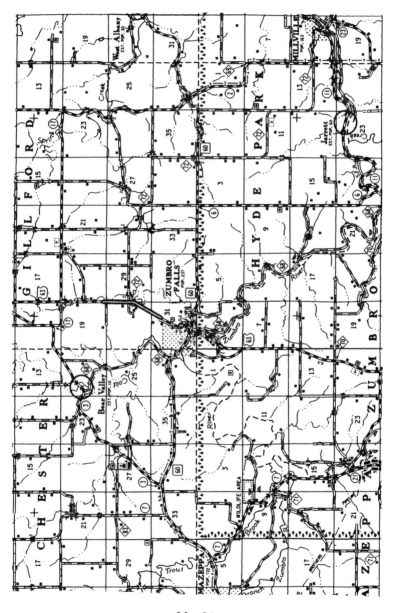

Map 24

Mazeppa Creek, marked "Trout Brook" on the county maps, flows five miles west of Cold Spring Brook on 60. It has more water than Cold Spring, but isn't quite as productive. This creek has its fans, however, so don't be surprised to find a vehicle or two parked at the bridge.

Continue west on Route 60 to Highway 52 near Zumbrota. Highway 52, as I've already mentioned, runs north to the Twin Cities and south through Rochester to Iowa. Go north on 52 to Route 58, then take 58 northeast to the little town of Haycreek on the banks of, you guessed it, Hay Creek.

Hay Creek meanders for more than a dozen miles from the big springs at the headwaters through a varied landscape of woods, meadow and pasture. There are plenty of bridges and access is very good (map 25).

If Hay Creek has a flaw, it is this popularity and easy access. Fishing pressure is heavy and many anglers discover that catching Hay Creek trout can be maddeningly difficult. It is a well-loved creek (despite the recent fish kill), and a place to visit often.

To find the creek, go south out of the town of Haycreek on Route 58 about a mile and go right, or west, on the unmarked lane. Follow this road to where it crosses Hay Creek. You can fish upstream or down from here, but an upstream trip can be rewarding in both fishing and scenery.

When you're done fishing, go back to the town of Haycreek the way you came. Follow Route 58 northeast into the city of Red Wing, a beautiful old river town with plenty of places to eat and stay. If you're camping, take Highway 61 southeast out of Red Wing about 9 miles to the scenic Frontenac State Park.

If you're returning to Rochester, take Route 58 southwest to Highway 52 and go south on 52 to Rochester.

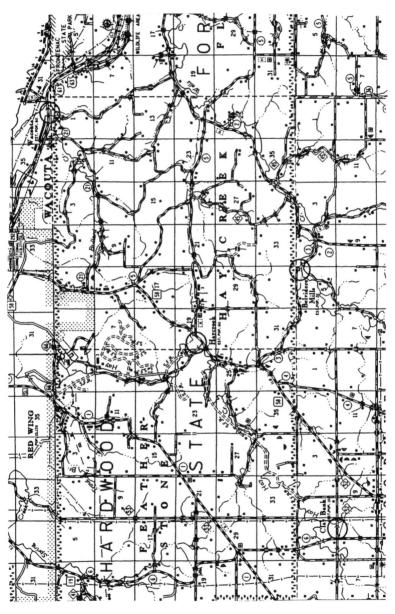

Map 25

THE LAST WORD

This brings us back to Rochester, where we began. Though we've covered several hundred miles, the streams highlighted in this guide represent barely more than half the designated trout streams in the southeast. I hope you'll find your way to the rest.

Remember, neither this guide nor the DNR map should be taken as the definitive list of trout streams in southeast Minnesota; many fine trout streams in the region are not designated as such by the DNR.

Good luck and good fishing.

APPENDIX

1. FOR MORE INFORMATION:

DNR Region V: Southeast-Fisheries Regional
Headquarters
2300 Silver Creek Road NE, Rochester, MN 55906
(507) 285-7427; fax (507) 285-7144

Fisheries Area Offices
Lake City - 801 South Oak Street, 55041
(612) 345-3365
Lanesboro - Route 2, Box 85, 55949
(507) 467-244
Or visit the DNR website at: www.dnr.state.mn.us

Minnesota Department of Tourism
Office of Tourism 800-657-3700
or call 296-5029 (in the Twin Cities)
Or at: www.exploreminnesota.com

2.   HOW TO REPORT POLLUTION

If you find evidence of pollution in one of southeast
Minnesota's streams, you should report its location as soon
as possible to the Minnesota Pollution Control Agency
(MPCA). Their address and phone numbers are listed
below:

MPCA Information Line
(612) 296-6300, or 800-657-3864
MPCA, 520 Lafayette Road, St. Paul, MN 55155-4194

MPCA 24-hour emergency number
(612) 649-5451 or 800-422-0798

Or, on the internet at: www.pca.state.mn.us

3.   CAMPING IN THE STATE PARKS:

For reservations, call 800-246-CAMP

Southeast Minnesota State Parks:

Beaver Creek Valley State Park: Forestville State Park:
(507) 724-2107   (507) 352-5111

Frontenac State Park: Whitewater State Park:
(612) 345-3401   (507) 932-3007

Great River Bluffs State Park
(formerly O.L. Kipp State Park):
(507) 643-6849

4. FOR MORE INFORMATION ON THE ROOT RIVER STATE TRAIL, WRITE TO:

Trail Center, Box 376, Lanesboro, MN 55949.
or call: (507) 467-2552.

Or contact the Minnesota Department of Natural Resources, Trails and Waterways Information Center at Box 40, 500 Lafayette Road, St. Paul, MN 55146. Or call (612) 296-6699 or 800-652-9747.

5. TURN IN POACHERS (TIP)

Statewide toll-free: 800-652-9093
24 hours a day, 365 days a year

6. TROUT UNLIMITED

1500 Wilson Blvd., Suite 310, Arlington VA 22209
(703) 522-0200

For more information on Minnesota Chapters of TU, visit TU online at: www.tu.org.

7. FEDERATION OF FLY FISHERS

P.O. Box 1595, 502 South 19th Ave., Bozeman, MT 59771
(406) 585-7592

SELECTED BIBLIOGRAPHY

Borger, Gary A.	*Naturals: A Guide to Food Organisms of the Trout.* Stackpole Books, 1980
Caucci, Al & Bob Nastasi	*Hatches II.* Lyons & Burford, 1991
Gierach, John	*Fly Fishing Small Streams.* Stackpole Books, 1989
Hughes, Jene	*Iowa Trout Streams.* Second Avenue Bait House, 1994
Humphrey, Jim & Bill Shogren	*Wisconsin & Minnesota Trout Streams.* W. W. Norton/Countryman Press, 1995
Karas, Nick	*Brook Trout.* Lyons & Burford Publishers, 1997
Knopp, Malcolm & Robert Cormier	*Mayflies.* Greycliff Publishing, 1997
LaFontaine, Gary	*The Dry Fly, New Angles.* Greycliff, 1990
	Trout Flies: Proven Patterns. Greycliff, 1993
	Caddisflies. Greycliff, 1981
Maclean, Norman	*A River Runs Through It.* University of Chicago Press, 1976
Mueller, Ross	*Upper Midwest Flies That Catch Trout.* R. Mueller Publications, 1995
Nemes, Sylvester	*The Soft-Hackled Fly.* Stackpole Books, 1993
Rosenbauer, Tom	*Reading Trout Streams.* Nick Lyons Books, 1988
Surber, Thaddeus	*A Biological Reconnaissance of the Root River Drainage Basin (appendix to the biennial report of the State Game and Fish Commissioner of Minnesota for the period ending June 30, 1924)*
van Vliet, John	*The Art of Fly Tying.* Cy DeCosse Inc., 1994
	Fly-Fishing Equipment & Skills. Cowles Media, 1996
	Fly Fishing for Trout in Streams, Subsurface Techniques. Cowles Media, 1996
Waters, Dr. Thomas	*Streams and Rivers of Minnesota.* University of Minnesota Press, 1977

Index of Streams